THE LATEST ON

Beta-carotene a newly recognized protector

Vitamin C new studies show even greater life-extending effects in patients

Vitamin E with C, now shown to block the formation of dangerous nitrosamines

Selenium an astonishing study of its hard-to-believe curative effects

These and other life-protecting cancer fighters can be used in your own program of cancer avoidance—and by physicians for increasingly effective treatment.

Richard Passwater has also written:

SUPERNUTRITION: Megavitamin Revolution

SUPERNUTRITION For Healthy Hearts

Super Calorie, Carbohydrate Counter

The Easy No-Flab Diet

Selenium as Food & Medicine

The Slendernow Diet

Guide to Fluorescence Literature, Volumes 1–3

Trace Minerals, Hair Analysis and Nutrition (with Elmer Cranton, M.D.)

He is also the co-editor of the Good Health Guide series.

Dr. Richard A. Passwater's
REVISED, UPDATED
FACT/BOOK ON

CANCER
AND ITS
NUTRITIONAL
THERAPIES

Keats Publishing, Inc.　　New Canaan, Connecticut

CANCER AND ITS NUTRITIONAL THERAPIES
Pivot Original Health Edition published 1978
Revised edition published 1983

Library of Congress Catalog Card Number: 78-57646
PIVOT ORIGINAL HEALTH BOOKS are published by
Keats Publishing, Inc.
27 Pine Street
New Canaan, Connecticut 06840

ACKNOWLEDGEMENTS

The dedication of a few intrepid researchers has brought us major advances that will prevent or reduce the suffering from cancer for many of us. My appreciation and thanks to them and others who have helped me in my research and to compile this book. Particularly I thank the following: Herb Boynton, Dr. Keith Brewer, Dr. Ewan Cameron, Dr. Ray Chen, Dr. Steve Cordas, Dr. Don Davis, John Ferguson, Dr. Carlton Fredericks, Dr. Doug Frost, Ken Halaby, Rick Hicks, Mort Katz, Dr. Hans Kugler, Dr. Harold Manner, Virgil Marsh, Wayne Martin, Dr. Hans Nieper, Dave Olson, Don Orlandi, Guido Orlandi, Jay Patrick, Dr. Linus Pauling, Dr. Miles Robinson, Irv Rosenberg, Dr. Gerhard Schrauzer, Fred Scott, Walt Seager, Ron Sell, Dr. Raymond Shamberger, Allen Skulnick, Harold Taub, Bill Wham, Dr. Roger Williams and Angus Wootten.
But most of all, Barbara.

CONTENTS

Preface

Cancer research holds special interest for me, as I have been over-exposed to all the known risk factors except smoking and obesity. Back in the days when most scientists thought cancer was caused by a virus, little concern was given to cancer-causing agents that have largely been banned from our environment today. My first five years as a chemist were spent as the supervisor of an instrumental analyses laboratory in a plant that made over one thousand chemicals, including several insecticides and a "nerve gas." The plant was located in a small town along the Delaware River in Pennsylvania that contained five oil refineries and numerous industrial plants, all within a few blocks of each other. Needless to say, the air was foul—the stench would stay on my clothes even when I left the area, and the water, well fortunately it was so foul-tasting, it couldn't be drunk. At the plant, we would always have to walk through clouds of dense gasses such as boron trifluoride or sulfur trioxide. The latter would mix with sweat to form sulfuric acid and eat small holes in my clothes. When the clothes were washed, they would fall apart because of the small holes—but that was good—it meant nobody could wear clothes too long. If they could have, the stench would be very noticeable, but worse, those chemicals would have been held against the skin in higher and higher concentrations.

I had extensive skin contact with solutions of the potent carcinogens benzapyrene and anthracene. I have had long-term exposure to an atmosphere largely consisting of the heated vapors of fire-ant pesticide and DDT, along with their solvents for analysis, carbon tetrachloride, carbon disulphide, chloroform, acetone and acetonitrile (methylcyanide).

Even worse, I operated a defective X-ray diffractometer, lacking shielding, and repeatedly received dangerous amounts of X-radiation. I'm sure it didn't help any that I am a red-haired and fair-skinned former sun worshiper, who drank a pint of a fruit drink colored with Red Dye No. 2 every day.

Fortunately during that time, I was lifting weights and taking a low-potency, vitamin tablet plus 100 I.U. of vitamin E daily. I only wish I had known the principles of Supernutrition and megavitamin therapy then.

That should give you an idea of why I research cancer prevention in my laboratory, and follow the research of others very closely. I have compiled my observations here so that they may help others. As our knowledge increases, it becomes apparent that we can avoid cancer, and many more people will be able to cure themselves of cancer. I hope this book helps in both respects.

Part One
SOME BASIC FACTS

CHAPTER 1

What the Healthy Body Can Do

A HEALTHY BODY can overcome cancer, just as it can ward off cancer. Those who disagree with this statement don't fully understand what a "healthy" body is. As our understanding of nutrition and health has advanced beyond the very obvious relationship of vitamin C and scurvy or vitamin B-1 and beriberi, there have been many experiments that demonstrate the role of vitamins and minerals in protecting the cells against the agents that cause cancer and in stimulating the immune response to destroy cancers. I will discuss these experiments in detail and suggest how this information can be applied to prevent, control or cure cancer.

Thus, *Cancer and Its Nutritional Therapies* is a practical guide to help prevent cancer and help those with cancer to get the most benefit out of their conventional therapy. The nutritional therapy, which brings the body to its peak of immune response, in no way conflicts with surgery, radiation, or chemotherapy. It is important to combine nutrition with conventional therapy, rather than try any single approach alone. Remember, cancer patients don't invariably die of cancer itself; they may die of complications such as infection and hemorrhage, which could be due to under-nutrition as much as to anything else.

Cancer is often described as a disease of civilization, but it will only strike when the body's defenses are down or when the cancer-causing agent is abnormally strong and its presence prolonged. Our strategy then should be to keep our defense up and to prevent un-necessary exposure to cancer-causing agents.

We can accomplish this with a few practical guide-lines, common sense and avoidance of extremes or fa-naticism. The Bible summarized this wisdom by "Let your moderation be known unto all men" (Philippians 4:5).

The body can withstand many different chemical in-sults, and as long as it is healthy, cancer will not de-velop until the body's pollutant-degradation system is overwhelmed. This is called the "Hockey Stick Princi-ple." Figure 1.1 shows a graph of cancer probability in relation to chemical pollution. There may be a thresh-old below which the healthy body can handle a given amount of pollutants. Many scientists believe this to be true, but concede it is virtually impossible to measure. Above that threshold, the cancer rate increases directly in relation to the concentration of pollutants. This re-sponse curve, flat at the bottom and then rising shar-ply, resembles the shape of a hockey stick.

Diversity in diet will help keep pollutants at a mod-erate level. In other words, eat many different kinds of food to "spread the poisons around" so that too much Red Dye No. 2, insecticides, DES or any pollutant does not become too concentrated in large amounts in your body. We will discuss many of the environmental and food pollutants and how to reduce exposure to them without becoming overly fanatical.

At one time, before modern civilization, man was nearly free of cancer. Even today several primitive cul-tures remain free of cancer, while the most "advanced"

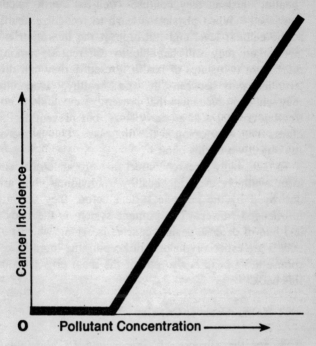

Fig. 1.1 Hockey Stick Principle. Some scientists believe the body can tolerate a certain level of pollution before risk of cancer increases.

civilizations have the highest per capita incidence of cancer.

Cancer has always been around but it was mostly the result of malnutrition combined with natural radiation, putrifaction of foods or exposure to environmental pollutants that existed even in some early societies.

Some will say that people didn't live long enough to develop cancer before this century. But enough did reach old age to make it noticeable that cancer was rare.

Others will argue that healthy people get cancer. They confuse "absence of obvious disease" with "health," just as they confuse "well-fed" with "well-nourished." When physicians learn to recognize health at the cellular level and nutrition at the micronutrient level, then they will be able to differentiate among more than two states of health. Presently they can differentiate only between "ill" and "healthy." Hopefully they will soon recognize that preventive medicine is not treating an illness at an early stage, but preventing the illness from developing in the first place. This is one of the objectives of this book.

In fact, many researchers feel that precancerous cells form routinely even in "healthy" individuals, but are destroyed by the immune system before they become full-fledged cancers. The immune system is the body's last line of defense against cancer. Learning which nutrients are especially helpful in keeping the immune response at its peak is also one of the main objectives of this book.

Not to Alarm or Criticize

It is not the purpose of *Cancer and Its Nutritional Therapies* to alarm readers with the increasing rate of cancer; nor is its objective to debate present treatments and research trends. That would only detract from the important information that cancer might well be prevented and often cured with good nutrition, and that the nutritional therapies described here are compatible with all other therapies.

I would like to emphasize the need for using nutritional therapy, however, since present methods have produced no improvement in the last twenty years.[1] In the 1950s, the overall five-year survival rate for white cancer patients was 39 percent; during 1960 to 1966, it was 40 percent; and for 1967-73, it was 41 percent. Thus in twenty years of so-called "great advances," the five-year survival rate has improved by 2 percent.

Perhaps even more unfortunately, the incidence of cancers of the type that respond most poorly to traditional therapies seem to be the ones on the increase.

Some researchers have concluded that the present conventional treatments of cancer only hasten suffering. Ivan Illich has said, "I do know that in the overwhelming majority of cancers, where a lot of money has been spent on diagnosis and therapy, neither the precocity of the diagnosis nor the kind of treatment used has any impact on the survival rates. We do have increasing evidence that those who are treated, supposedly for curative purposes, at best have an earlier onset of anguish, a prolonged period of impairment, and a greater intensity of pain than those who succeed in escaping the doctor."[2]

I didn't quote that to discourage anyone from using conventional treatment. That is another issue which in my opinion is not ready for judgment at this time. I quoted Dr. Illich to demonstrate that those physicians who may still reject the fact that nutritional therapies are effective are themselves standing on shaky ground. They should be eager to add to their arsenal of weapons against cancer, but instead they often reveal their ignorance of modern nutritional research and attempt to discourage their patients from taking vitamin supplements.

You alone are responsible for your health. Your physician is your partner in health matters, but you are the boss. It will be your job to show your physician the evidence here that I hope will prove the role of nutrients in controlling cancer.

Allow me just one more quotation to make my point that present therapies alone are not the final answer, and that there is a need to add nutritional therapy.

Dr. Hardin Jones of the University of California Department of Medical Physics reports: "My studies have proven conclusively that untreated cancer victims actually live up to four times longer than treated individuals. For a typical type of cancer, people who refused treatment lived for an average of twelve and a half years. Those who accepted surgery and other kinds of treatment lived an average of only three years. . . . I attribute this to the traumatic effect of surgery on the body's natural defense mechanisms. The body has a natural defense against every type of cancer.

"Medical treatment seems to interfere with and mess up this natural resistance. You see, it is not the cancer that kills the victim; it's the breakdown of the defense mechanism that eventually brings death.

"With every cancer patient who keeps in excellent physical shape and boosts his health to build up his natural resistance, there is a high chance the body will find its own defense against the cancer."[3]

This book will give practical guidance to maintain the body's defense mechanism at its peak with supernutrition, so that if you decide on surgery, radiation or chemotherapy, the "cure" will not weaken your body below its needed defense requirements.

War on Cancer

The increase in cancer rate that has resulted because of increased environmental and food pollution has prompted the "war on cancer" initiated in 1971. The "war on cancer" may have been a good political move, and even have the side effect of being a fund raiser for the American Cancer Society. But it seems it promised the public more than it could deliver. As a result, the public has become disillusioned with the establishment's efforts to find a miracle cure rather than consider prevention and nutrition. The official blundering of the Laetrile matter has also seriously annoyed the public. By 1975, two billion dollars had been spent through the National Cancer Act of 1971, and by 1978 no significant results had yet been brought forth. Yet, when cured cancer victims report that they were helped by nutritional therapy, the physicians and cancer researchers laugh. We have paid for all of this fruitless research and cover-up; isn't it time to increase research efforts into nutritional therapies? Public pressure must be brought to bear upon those controlling the funding for such programs.

Will we continue to allow more than 90 percent of the tax dollars used for cancer research that tries to find cancer viruses and develops poisonous drugs as "therapy," when we already know that at least 90 percent of cancers are caused by environmental and food pollutants? Have we forgotten the wisdom of the adage, "an ounce of prevention is worth a pound of cure"? Or should we ask if our funding system is controlled by scientists held in high esteem by their peers because they are professionals whose whole scientific underpinning has been toward early diagnosis and treating disease rather than toward prevention?

References

1. Frei, Emil. *New England J. Med.*, 293: 3, 147, 17 July 1975. Cutler, Sidney J., *et al. New England J. Med.*, 293: 3, 122, 1975. Greenberg, Daniel S. *Columbia Journalism Review*, February 1975. Greenberg, Daniel S. *Science*, 293: 26, 1279-1380, 1975.

2. Illich, Ivan. *Washington Star*. 27 May 1975.

3. Jones, Hardin. Lecture at the American Cancer Society's Annual Science Writers' Conference. New Orleans, 7 March 1969.

CHAPTER 2

The Nature
of the Beast

CANCER is a family of diseases that seem to be best characterized as "uncontrolled growth." There are three basic types of cancer; carcinomas, sarcomas and leukemia-like cancers.

The most common cancers are the carcinomas, which are malignant tumors that occur in the epithelial cells that cover tissues and line body cavities, and in glandular organs such as the breast. Cancers of the mouth, stomach, lungs, prostate and gastro-intestinal tract would be classified as carcinomas.

Sarcomas are less common, but highly malignant. They form in connective tissues, muscle, bone and cartilage.

Leukemia-like cancers include: (1) leukemia, which results from the overproduction of white blood cells, followed by their underproduction; (2) lymphomas, tumors in lymphoid tissue which cause the overproduction of lymphoid cells (cells found in bone marrow from which all blood cells are thought to arise); and (3) multiple myelomas, a bone-marrow tumor, which is the rarest form of cancer, that causes the overproduction of plasma cells.

An adult who has cancer will most often have a carcinoma, while young children most often have leukemia.

The reason that I make an issue of the different classes of cancers is that they are definitely different in kind. In other words, they respond differently to drugs because of their different patterns of development and growth.

I also make an issue of the three classifications of cancer because scientists are studying the wrong class. Besides chasing viruses, which cannot account for more than a few percent of cancers, if for any human cancers at all, emphasis has been placed on the sarcoma types of cancer, although we know the vast majority (more than 90 percent) of cancers are carcinomas. Why?

I suspect it has to do with a scientist's preference for working with the broadest base of knowledge possible and the wide availability of tissue cultures that can produce sarcomas.

It is very difficult to obtain and grow the pure epithelial cells needed for growing carcinomas. They are not commercially available. Thus, scientists must spend a lot of time and hard work just to get to first base in their research, and yet we have a tendency to judge scientists by the number of their publications.

On the other hand, fibroblast cells, like 3T3 and W138, that lead to sarcomas grow easily in simple bottles and are commercially available at low cost. The cancers produced by these two types of cells are vastly different. So we gain little from the increased amount of research on the rarest forms of cancer.

To compound the issue even more, the 3T3 cell line has abnormal chromosomal conditions that make it not even a good line to follow in cancer research.

Furthermore, there is evidence that much of the commercially available cell lines have been contaminated with other cells, and the cultures grown have actually been different from what the scientist thought they were. In 1974 Dr. Walter Nelson-Rees located 102 separate instances, totaling more than forty erroneous identifications of cell cultures. The cells were all HeLa instead of whatever the researchers thought they had.[1]

But talk to these scientists about varying nutrients in the growth media they culture their tissues in and you get nowhere.

Is it any wonder that hundreds of nutritional advances against cancer have been published in the scientific literature around the world, but have been ignored and even suppressed? Nutrition hasn't been in vogue among the scientists who have risen to the top of the cancer research hierarchy of virus and fibroblast-tissue culture experts.

The times are slowly changing, as brave environmental cancer experts are gaining a greater voice in the newspapers to bring public pressure upon the program administrators. The same pressures must be brought upon the establishment in behalf of nutritional therapies. All other therapies seem doomed without proper nutrition, and I believe nutritional therapy alone would bring about a higher cure rate than conventional therapy alone now does. The goal, of course, is to combine the best of all therapies.

Major Cancers

The majority of cancers are caused, in my opinion, by chemical damage to cell membranes or by damaged DNA, either of which leads to cell mutation. A precancerous cell is a mutated cell that, upon further growth or division, leads to a full-fledged cancer unless the mutated cells are recognized as such by the immune system and destroyed.

The cell membrane is the protective outer skin of a cell that is responsible for the transport of nutrients into the cell and the removal of waste products. The cell membrane also contains sensors for detecting the proximity of neighboring cells and controls the production of more cells.

If the cell membrane is damaged, then nutrients might not enter the cell and cellular death may result, or cancer-causing chemicals may enter the cell and initiate DNA damage. If the cell membrane is damaged at a site of a sensor that regulates cellular reproduction, uncontrolled growth may result.

Under the powerful electron-scanning microscope, normal cells are relatively flat and orderly. When they are grown on glass plates in a laboratory, they cover the plate in a thick, flat sheet only one cell thick. But cancer cells climb atop other cancer cells in an eerie, disorderly pattern of clumps and bumps.

Normal cells stop growing when they meet neighboring cells, but cancer cells keep on growing uncontrollably. Their cell-to-cell communication has been destroyed and they no longer respect each others' boundaries.

This type of cell membrane damage can arise from highly reactive fragments of molecules called "free radicals." A free radical is like a delegate at a convention—it will react with the first thing that comes along. It is an atom or group of atoms possessing an odd (unpaired) electron. Most free radicals are extremely reactive because of their tendency to gain (capture) an additional electron and thus be complete.

When a free radical is formed, energy is supplied to the fragment during its cleavage from the parent molecule, and this energy-rich fragment tends strongly to lose energy by the formation of a new chemical bond. Free radicals generally initiate chain reactions, producing more free radicals and reacted products. One free radical can produce chain reactions altering thousands and thousands of molecules.

A free radical is not to be confused with a charged ion. A free radical can react with the membrane and in the process produce additional free radicals in the unsaturated fatty acids in the membrane which, if unchecked by adequate amounts of vitamin E, will produce more and more damage.

Free-radical damage to DNA is critical. DNA (deoxyribo-nucleic acid) is the material in living matter that reproduces itself and forms all of the materials and cells of life. There is one important exception: those nearly fifty essential nutrients that can be taken into the body only through diet.

If DNA becomes damaged, it can make the abnormal cells that become cancer. Free radicals are routinely produced in the body and are held in check by antiradical nutrients such as vitamins A, C and E, and minerals such as selenium. The number of free radicals can become elevated whenever there is a deficiency in the antiradical (antioxidant) nutrients or too much is consumed of free-radical-producing pollutants such as smog, chlorine in water, certain food additives, or benzopyrene in cigarette smoke. It is only reasonable that protection against cancer dictates limited exposure to these pollutants and increased intake of protective nutrients.

Free radicals can be formed as a reaction to unneeded superoxidation in the cell (peroxidation), or as a reaction to insufficient oxygen. Nobel Laureate (1931) Dr. Otto Warburg long ago noted that normal cells use oxygen-based reactions as their source of energy, but cancer cells can form from cells not receiving adequate oxygen. These oxygen-deficient cells sometimes change to a glucose-based chemistry to derive their source of energy instead of dying. If the cells make this switch, they become cancer cells. Some scientists believe that cancer cells can be made to switch back when they are given adequate amounts of oxygen, but this remains unproven.

It does seem logical to assume that those nutrients that help provide cells with oxygen, such as vitamin E and the B-complex vitamins, will lessen the number and possibility of normal cells becoming cancer cells.

But even if pre-cancerous cells or a large tumor do form, our immune response, if kept in super-healthy condition, may help destroy the cancer.

Lung Cancer

Ninety percent of lung cancer victims are smokers. The remaining 10 percent probably breathe heavy amounts of polluted air or other people's smoke. Chances are good that this type of cancer could be drastically reduced if more people stopped smoking and air pollution were cleared up.

Breast Cancer

Dr. Carlton Fredericks has written a book called *Breast Cancer: A Nutritional Approach* (Grosset and Dunlap, N.Y., 1977). In his book, Dr. Fredericks explains the relationship between breast cancer and excessive levels of estrogen. The B-complex vitamins help convert estrogens to estriol.

Breast cancer patients have lower levels of estriol than normal. Estriol levels are elevated during pregnancy, and women who become pregnant at an early age, say before twenty-five, have up to a 50 percent lower risk of breast cancer.

Studies have shown that those women most prone to breast cancer are those with a family history of breast cancer, women who have been overweight for a long time and probably were obese as teenagers, those who have never been pregnant, and those with smaller breasts.

A seven-year test involving 7,214 women was conducted by Dr. John N. Wolfe of Hutzel Hospital in Detroit. He found the risk of breast cancer for women with the smallest breasts was 446 per 1000, but for women with the larger breasts, the risk was only 14.5 per 1000 women. That's a thirty-fold difference.[2]

Dr. Wolfe made the following risk classifications:

Lowest risk: Big breasts composed primarily of fat with no or small amounts of fibrous tissue, and no visible ducts. Rate of risk: 14.5 women per 1000.

Low risk: Fairly large breasts, chiefly fat, with prominent ducts in the back portion taking up to a quarter of the breast size. Rate of risk: 38.5 women per 1000.

High risk: Smaller breasts with prominent ducts taking up more than a quarter of breast size. Rate of risk: 175 women per 1000.

Highest risk: Smallest breasts and very often severe fibrous cysts obscured by prominent duct pattern, until age 55 or 60 when fat tissue disappears. Rate of risk: 446 women per 1000.

Women often discover "lumps" in their breasts and fear cancer. Some of these lumps are merely sacs of fluid also containing fibrous growth—i.e. fibrous cysts. These are regarded by some physicians as possible precursors to cancer, or at least risk factors that bear watching. However, no one has ever proved that fibrous cysts inevitably change to cancer.

Vitamin E has been used successfully by many physicians to make fibrous cysts disappear. The mechanism is not known as to how vitamin E does this. It may be through a prostaglandin reaction as in peridontal disease which also involves sacs.

Additional factors associated with breast cancer development are deficiencies in the minerals iodine and selenium. They will be discussed in their respective chapters, as will the involvement of vitamin E deficiency.

Colonic-Rectal Cancers

These cancers have been traced in many cases to deficiencies of fiber in the diet and of antioxidant nutrients such as vitamins C and E. Each of these factors will be discussed in their respective chapters.

Skin Cancer

Skin cancer is one of the forms of cancer most noticeably on the increase. The risk can be controlled essentially by reducing exposure to the sun by wearing protective clothing—especially wide-brimmed hats—and using sunscreens that contain PABA, one of the B-complex vitamins. Vitamins C and E also help limit the sun's damage.

A Brief Review of Some of the Major Causes of Cancer

This list is an over-simplification, of course, and is not meant to put all blame on any specific item. For example, if a friend has cervical cancer, don't assume she had early sex with multiple sex partners. This list merely means that the cancer rate in large groups would be reduced if the associated risk factors were reduced.

- Lung Cancer—cigarette smoking
- Colon Cancer—low-fiber diet
- Cervical Cancer—early sex with multiple partners; poor personal hygiene
- Stomach Cancer—eating cooked foods left unrefrigerated

- Uterine Cancer—taking estrogens after menopause
- Esophageal Cancer—heavy alcohol consumption combined with cigarette smoking
- Bladder Cancer—industrial carcinogens; smoking
- Breast Cancer—mineral deficiencies; obesity
- Skin Cancer—overexposure to sun
- Lip Cancer—pipe and cigar smoking

Of course, many people believe that improved nutrition will do as much, or more, to lower the incidence of cancer as avoiding the chemical carcinogens. But do both.

References

1. Nelson-Rees, Walter, Flandermeyer, Robert R. and Hawthorne, Paula K. *Science,* 184: 1093-1096, 7 June 1974. *Also see:* Culliton, B. J. *Science,* 184: 1056-1059, 7 June 1974.

2. Wolfe, John N. *Am. J. Roentgenology, Radium Therapy and Nuclear Therapy,* 126:6, 1130-1139, June 1976.

1983 UPDATE

Breast Size and Type

The validity of Dr. Wolfe's breast-type patterns is far from a settled issue, but there are more confirmational studies than invalidating. A second explanation implies that it is just easier to detect small tumors in some breast types (MWN 31, 12/79.)

Ruined Studies

Many more cancer studies must now be ruled invalid because of improper cell lines or mouse strains being used. Dr. Nelson-Rees too asks, "Isn't anyone working with the right cells?" (Michael Gold in the April *Science 81*; also *Science* 209, 720, 8 Aug 1980.)

CHAPTER 3

First Line
of Defense

MANY scientists believe, perhaps with good reason, that cancer results when the body's immune system fails. There is some evidence that quite regularly cells grow wildly, but are detected and destroyed by the immune system.

Defective cells constructed with proteins produced by altered DNA, or cells with defective membranes, can grow uncontrollably. As long as nutrients are available, these cells will continue to grow and divide irregularly. Normally, antibodies are summoned which surround and isolate the premalignant cells and, with the help of macrophages (large scavenger cells), destroy them. If the body does not detect the premalignant cells as foreign, or cannot produce adequate antibodies, or if the antibodies are blocked before they do their job, then the cells develop their own blood supply and become malignant tissue.

The stimulation of the immune system is receiving increasing interest as a cure for cancer. Surgery, radiation and chemotherapy techniques are only effective, as a rule, when the cancer has been detected early. Several medical researchers have been successful in stimulating antibody formation with smallpox or the antituberculosis vaccine, Bacillus Calmette-Guerin (BCG), and they have cured or brought about remission of cancer.

The immune system is a complicated and poorly understood defense mechanism. It can destroy cancer unless it's weakened by poor nutrition, emotional strain or by "blocking factors" formed in advanced cancers. If the body is well nourished, the immune response will still be able to destroy cancers even under emotional strain, and there will be no advanced cancers to form "blocking factors."

The immune system defends the body against bacteria, viruses and other foreign invaders, as well as mis-formed materials in the body. It quickly recognizes, attacks, and destroys all foreign bodies that can harm.

Lymphocytes are a particular variety of white blood cell that typically make up 25 to 30 percent of all white blood cells. They can be distinguished from the typical white cells under a microscope by their lack of granules. Lymphocytes are made in the thymus (a small glandular organ in the neck and upper part of chest behind the breastbone that becomes dormant after puberty), but primarily they are made in bone marrow. After their formation, lymphocytes are transported to the lymph nodes and spleen for lifetime storage to be used when needed. Major lymph nodes are under the arms, in the groin, behind the ears, and in the abdominal cavity and a few other places. These white blood cells are released in response to infection.

But even before the supply of lymphocytes is released in the body to fight infection, the available lymphocytes react immediately to any threat by releasing proteins called antibodies. After antibodies attack the invader, larger cells called macrophages are summoned to "chew up" the invader.

Both antibodies and lymphocytes are released in response to the presence of cancerous cells. Dr. Ronald B. Herberman of the National Cancer Institute has measured the formation of antibodies and lymphocytes in mice that have been injected with "cancer virus."[1]

Leukemia patients also produce both antibodies and lymphocytes. They are probably the cause of the remissions that so dramatically occur in many people with their illness. And when these antibodies and lymphocytes disappear, the patient relapses into leukemia again.

When cancers form they release proteins and sugars called cancer antigens. These antigens are thought by some scientists to contaminate cell membranes in such a way as to convert that cell to a cancer cell, or the cancer antigens may tie up antibodies and lymphocytes in some way so as to prevent their appropriate action. This is a blocking factor that prevents the body from overcoming the cancer.

An important consideration is that additional antibodies or lymphocytes can even unblock antibody-antigen complexes, and the cancer can be destroyed. However, if the cancer is protected long enough, it develops its own protection system that can destroy macrophages.

Thus a healthy immune system, or possibly even fresh injections of someone's stored lymphocytes, can overcome cancer in a person previously having a weakened immune system.

There is considerable evidence for the relationship between some cancers and a weakened immune system. In studies by Dr. Robert S. Schwartz of the New England Medical Center and Dr. Martin S. Hirsch of the Massachusetts General Hospital, it has been shown that organ transplant patients given immunosuppressant drugs to prevent rejection of their new organ by their bodies have a higher than normal incidence of cancer.[2] However, they were mostly the rarer cancers.

As mentioned earlier, researchers have been successful in stimulating the immune response with standard smallpox or BCG vaccines and have reported cures and remissions in animals. Not all cancer patients have weak immune responses to bacteria or viruses. It may be that the immune system was simply overwhelmed with massive amounts of carcinogens or weak at the onset of the cancer, and the cancer developed its own ability to destroy macrophages, block antibodies and to "mask" itself so as not to be recognized as an "invader" by the body until too late.

Another explanation is that the immune response senses cancer cells differently from other invaders, but there is no evidence to support this. The best clue lies in the fact that in cancer patients having normal amounts of antibodies, the antibodies and macrophages contain abnormally low concentration levels of vitamin C.

The best hope remains in always retaining a strong immune response, while at the same time trying to avoid carcinogens. Daily supernutrition and a positive attitude are crucial to a peak immune response.

References

1. Herberman, Ronald B. *Science News*, 103: 408, 23 June 1973.

2. Schwartz, Robert. *Progress in Clinical Immunology*, Vol. 2. New York: Academic Press, 1975. Hirsch, Martin S. *Progress in Clinical Immunology*, Vol. 2, New York: Academic Press, 1975.

CHAPTER 4

Common Sense Ways
of Avoiding Cancer

MOST authorities will agree that between 75 and 90 percent of human cancers are caused by carcinogens (cancer-causing substances) in the environment, or excessive exposure to radiation. As time goes by, more and more scientists revise their figures upward, as more and more is learned about what is in the environment.

As the dangers are identified, risk of cancer can be reduced by cutting back exposure to each known carcinogen. There are between 70,000 and 100,000 chemicals known to be in the environment, and approximately 1,000 new ones are added each year. It is reasonable to expect that 1,000 to 1,500 of these chemicals are carcinogenic.

The public used to learn of a new carcinogen each month, but even though the Environmental Protection Agency has only 100 scientists looking for toxic chemicals in the environment, one month in 1977 brought about the disclosure of four dangers—Tris, Fyrol, DBCP and permanent hair dyes. And the dangers are turning out to be chemicals in wide usage such as saccharin.

However, there are more carcinogens yet to be identified, so we must live by the principle of moderation in all things. Don't eat or drink *anything* excessively.

On the other hand, it does no good—and only harm—to worry about the hidden dangers about which nothing can be done. Fanatical avoidance of every possible carcinogen is not possible. They are everywhere. But be reasonable about avoiding unnecessary exposure to proven strong carcinogens.

For example, food colors such as Red Dye No. 2 have been shown to be carcinogenic, at least at some level, in animals. It is not necessary that maraschino cherries be bright red. Develop a preference for the natural white maraschino cherry—it's available.

Roughly half of all cancer deaths are due to lung cancer, large-intestine cancer, and breast cancer. Lung cancer is the greatest single cause of cancer deaths, yet it can largely be eliminated by not smoking. A smoker increases the risk of dying anywhere from tenfold to fiftyfold, depending on the amount smoked and the length of time the person has smoked.

Cancer of the large intestine may be inversely related to the amount of antioxidants in the diet (the less antioxidant, the more free radicals, and the higher the incidence of cancer) or the amount of roughage (the more roughage in the diet, the faster the waste material moves along the bowel, and the less chance of putrefaction and the development of free radicals).

Breast cancer may be related to deficiencies of the B-vitamins and the minerals selenium and iodine.

The fact that some religious groups such as the Mormons and Seventh-day Adventists have much lower cancer rates than the United States average, strongly suggests that moderation in lifestyle and the avoidance of smoking and alcohol can be a major factor in preventing cancer. Both these groups are close knit and advocate temperance and moderation in all things. However, notice that I don't suggest vegetarianism.

The overall incidence of colonic and rectal cancer in Mormons living in Utah is below that reported for the Seventh-day Adventists living in California, who claim a 50 percent compliance with a vegetarian diet.[1] The Mormon Church has never advocated any form of vegetarianism, nor preached abstention from the use of meat. The Utah Beef Council reports the per capita beef consumption of 59 kilograms per year in Utah (which also has a lower colonic and rectal cancer rate than the Seventh-day Adventists) as compared to 52 kilograms per year in the United States in 1972. So, the Mormons eat more beef than the average American, yet have a lower colonic rectal and overall cancer rate than the Seventh-day Adventists of whom 50 percent are vegetarians.

It would seem that some old-fashioned "bad habits" can increase the risk of cancer. Dr. Marvin Schneiderman of the National Cancer Institute reports that people who smoke and drink large amounts of alcohol run an increased risk of dying from head, neck or esophogeal cancers. It appears that alcohol is a co-carcinogen that potentiates (strengthens) the carcinogenic effect of tobacco smoke.

Ten Major Causes of Cancer

The ten major causes of cancer begin to evolve as the following:
1) Smoking
2) Occupational pollutants
3) Excessive sunlight and X-radiation
4) Pesticides, animal growth hormones and food additives
5) Water pollution, excess chlorine, chlorinated compounds and fluorides in drinking water
6) Undernutrition and lack of dietary fiber
7) Air pollution

8) Heavy drinking of alcohol
9) Some drugs used as medicine
10) Negative or suppressed emotions and attitudes

A brief look at each of these causes will help identify the major risks involved.

Smoking

Tobacco smoke is the number one controllable cause of cancer. More than 40 percent of cancers in men, and between 25 and 30 percent of cancers in women, are related to cigarette smoking. Smoking causes mouth, throat and bladder cancers as well as lung cancer.

Dr. Alton Ochsner, founder of the famous Ochsner Clinic in New Orleans, called tobacco the greatest health hazard in the United States. Emerson Foote, a member of the National Interagency Council on Smoking and Health, in testifying before a Congressional Committee, stated that 360,000 persons died in a recent year in the United States because of tobacco use.

Dr. E. C. Hammond of the National Cancer Institute (and vice-president of the American Cancer Society in 1976) commented in 1969 that 447,196 men born between 1868 and 1927 and still living on July 1, 1960, had an estimated lifespan at age 35 of 42.4 years for men who had never smoked, 37.8 years for men who smoked 1 to 9 cigarettes daily, 37.1 years for those who smoked 10 to 19 cigarettes daily, 36.5 years for those who smoked 20 to 39 cigarettes daily, and 34.7 years for those smoking two packs or more daily.[2]

So two-pack-a-day smokers lose eight years of life. These smokers often rationalize that they don't need those "old-age" years. The truth is that not only do the heavy smokers lose years of life, they lose life from their years. They increase their suffering and move the crippling diseases forward in time so that they get "old-age" afflictions at middle age. And ladies—this includes facial wrinkles. A two-pack-a-day smoker at thirty years has the facial wrinkles of a non-smoker of forty.

Until the mid-1930s, lung cancer was an extremely rare disease. However, during World War I, men began to smoke heavily, and the vitamin E content of our diet decreased because of new refining methods for flour. In 1930 there were 2,500 lung cancer deaths; in 1950, 16,000; in 1956, 29,000; in 1964, 43,100; in 1974, 75,500; and in 1976, 81,000. A thirty-two fold increase.

The lung cancer death rate has climbed from less than 3 per 100,000 population to more than 40 per 100,000. During this time cancer has risen from twelfth to second among causes of death in the United States.

Dr. Alton Oschner relates, "I first became aware of the possible relationship between cigarette smoking and cancer of the lung in 1936. In 1919, during my junior year at Washington University, a patient with cancer of the lung was admitted to the Barnes Hospital. As was usual, the patient died. Dr. George Dock, our Professor of Medicine, who was not only an eminent clinician and scientist but also an excellent pathologist, insisted upon the two senior classes witnessing the autopsy, and he stressed that *the condition was so rare he thought we might never see another case as long as we lived.* (Emphasis added.) Being young and impressionable, I was very much impressed by the rarity of this condition. I did not see another case until 1936 when, at Charity Hospital in New Orleans, I saw nine cases in six months. Having been impressed with its rarity by Dr. Dock seventeen years previously, I wondered what was responsible for this apparent epidemic."[3]

Of course, nonsmokers get lung cancer too. About

10 percent of all cases of lung cancer occur in non-smokers. This is easily explained by occupational pollution, air pollution, undernutrition, and the ridiculous fact that even those who choose not to smoke have to breathe the carcinogens put in the air by smokers. Still only one nonsmoker in every 3,300 men aged fifty-five and older dies from lung cancer whereas one in every forty chain smokers dies of this disease—an eighty-one times greater risk.

Everyone pays for the economic loss—the 100 million man-days lost because of tobacco-related illness, the 306 million work-days of partial disability—amounting to 19 billion dollars in 1965. How about the hospital expense of those dying of lung cancer? I'd rather pay them Social Security.

I know a lot of nice, otherwise intelligent, people who may have done only one stupid thing in their lives—get hooked on smoking. My advice: quit today. If you can't, cut back and be sure to take extra amounts of vitamins A, B-15, C and E. The reason for this will be explained in later chapters.

Occupational Pollutants

Occupational pollutants refer to those materials used on the job. Of course, these same pollutants often get into the air and water to pollute others, but the repeated direct exposure of highly concentrated carcinogens on the job is particularly deadly.

Workers so exposed can help save their lives by wearing protective clothing and masks.

There are now strict limits on the industrial exposure to asbestos in quarries and factories, but how about in office buildings full of asbestos particles from ceiling tiles?

The same is true for the manufacture of polyvinylchloride, but how about those that heat-seal polyvinyl packages?

There have been over 1,000 chemicals shown to cause cancer in animals, of which nearly forty have been shown to cause cancer in man already. Scan the list at the end of this chapter and see if you use, eat or make any of these products (read the labels of everything you use or eat). If you do, check with your company's health or safety officer or the nearest office of the Occupational Safety and Health Administration (OSHA).

Recently, it has been found that workers' clothing brings the danger home to the rest of the family as well. If you work with chemicals, try to keep your work clothes at work and wash them separately.

Excessive Sun and X-radiation

Next to lung cancer, the incidence of skin cancer is increasing the most rapidly. Ninety-eight percent of skin cancer is due to overexposure to the sun. Fair-skinned people should forget about trying to tan—besides it speeds the onset of wrinkling. All people should wear hats or caps while gardening, fishing, golfing or during any exposure to the sun for more than one-half hour. Excessively deep tans should be avoided by all. PABA, one of the B-complex vitamins, should be worn as a sunscreen; it is available in pure or diluted form in many sun lotions and creams—read the label.

Animal experiments show that nuclear radiation and x-irradiation can increase cancer incidence and mimic the aspect of aging. Strong doses cause whole-cell destruction leading to radiation sickness and death. Localized strong doses are used to destroy cancerous cells. All cells are destroyed, but cancer cells are preferentially killed since highly proliferating cells have more rapid DNA synthesis, which in turn are more vulnerable to attack by radiation. Lesser doses do damage indirectly by creating free radicals and disrupting lysosomal membranes which allow destructive lysosomal enzymes to leak out and damage the cell interior.

The free radicals initiated by radiation can thus do damage that leads to cancer, or by disrupting lysosomal membranes destroy cells, accelerating the aging process.

Forget about annual chest X rays, unless you are a smoker or have some symptoms requiring a chest X ray. Don't permit X rays just out of medical curiosity or as protection against possible malpractice suits. If an X ray is absolutely necessary, take vitamin E first if you can.

Pesticides, Hormones and Additives in Food

The FDA says one day that Red Dye No. 2 is safe, and the next day it's banned as a carcinogen. The FDA Commissioner tells us one day that foods free of pesticides are no better than foods with pesticides; and the next day the Environmental Protection Agency bans more pesticides as being carcinogenic. DES is a known carcinogenic yet traces still appear in some foods. There is enough PCP (pentachlorophenol) in our food supply to cause hundreds of thousands of cancers in the next ten to fifteen years. The so-called "safe" foods contain many untested additives, growth hormones and pesticides. What is worse is that no one has ever tested the effect of combinations of additives in our food. There is growing evidence that some additives do potentiate the toxicity of others, and perhaps potentiate their carcinogency as well.

For example, the oral toxic dose (LD-50) of butylated hydroxytoluene (BHT) is lowered by combined administration with alkylbenzenesulfonate (LAS).

Think what can happen when the various food additives, growth hormones and contaminants are ingested by a heavy smoker and drinker. Dr. E. Cuyler Hammond, vice-president of the American Cancer Society, says "much or perhaps most human cancer is caused not by single carcinogenic agents, but by interaction of multiple factors to which people are exposed."[4]

Hardly a day goes by without some clever food technologist coming up with a new food additive, sometimes just a little different from a banned additive, but different enough to get around the ban.

As air, wind and water transport chemicals around the earth, DDT shows up at the poles; traces of the defoliants used in the Vietnam war show up in grains in the American Midwest. I have detected very low traces of the carcinogen TCDD (Tetrachlorodibenzo-p-dioxin) in grains with an extremely sensitive instrument called a spectrophotoflurometer. Perhaps not enough to get alarmed about, but it proves that unless chemicals degrade rapidly to safe compounds, they come back to haunt us. Technically, those grains contaminated with the slight trace of TCDD would have to be removed from the food supply under the Delaney clause.

With the attack on the valuable Delaney clause by the saccharin fans (another mild carcinogen) I decided not to press the issue. I would hate to think what would happen to our foods without the Delaney clause.

By now it should be obvious that we can't avoid all carcinogens. In spite of the synergistic or potentiating effect of combinations of pollutants, it is best to diversify food intake in order to keep any one poison at a low level; the diet should have sufficient nutrients to keep the liver healthy, so that it will destroy the carcinogens before damage occurs.

Water Pollution, Chlorine and Fluoride

The Environmental Protection Agency has warned that much of the water supplies come from streams that are sewers for agricultural pesticides and industrial wastes. In addition, the anti-bacterial chlorine produces free radicals which can cause cancer and form other chlorine-family carcinogens such as chloroform and carbon tetrachloride.

The best protection is the intake of vitamin E and the use of activated-carbon water purifiers for drinking (and even bathing) water. A water-still can be used if it is one that allows you the rejection of the lighter boiling chloroform-type compounds and you replace the minerals that are removed.

Dr. Linus Pauling has found that a few grains of vitamin C added to a glass of water will cause the chlorine to bubble out in a few seconds. If a swimming pool is chlorinated, try not to swim the same day that you add the chlorine. The case against fluoride is also increasingly convincing. Why should that chemical be forced on everyone? The people who want it can put it directly on their own teeth. Many people have headaches, but we shouldn't put aspirin in the drinking water, should we?

Undernutrition and Lack of Dietary Fiber

These are the main theses of this book and will be dealt with in detail later.

Air Pollution

Smog and industrial air pollution are well known as causes of cancer. A high cancer rate occurs among those people living downwind of smelters and certain factories, and close to major highways.

The air is often polluted with oxidizing chemicals such as ozone and nitrous oxide. These compounds are present in smog and do harm to the body in at least two ways: (1) they directly oxidize lung tissue, causing disease and reducing the body's ability to abstract oxygen from the air; (2) the oxidizing chemicals destroy the vitamin A in the lung tissue, thereby increasing the risk of cancer. Vitamin A is needed for the health of the mucous membrane of the lung. Even if the vitamin A intake seems adequate, the lungs become deficient because of the oxidizing chemicals in the air. That is, unless the lungs are protected by extra vitamin E. Vitamin E, an antioxidant, can protect the lung tissues, including tissue stores of vitamin A.

In 1970, I filed a patent showing how vitamin E and other antioxidants protected lungs against air pollution. The amount of protection increased directly with the amount of antioxidant and to a degree with the length of time of taking the antioxidants prior to exposure to the smog. An important distinction to note is that these studies showed that vitamin E was progressively effective even beyond basic nutritional requirements; this, even though other scientists have implied that vitamin E would be effective only as it corrected nutritional deficiencies.

During exposure to moderate smog, it is projected that an *extra* 400 I.U. of vitamin E is indicated. Additional vitamin A and vitamin C are also needed.

Alcohol

Alcohol has been shown to be a co-carcinogen. It doesn't cause cancer itself, but it potentiates other carcinogens such as tobacco smoke. The principle of moderation applies here.

The "Pill" and Other Drugs

Some drugs have been linked to tumors and cancer, including the birth control pill, a hormone replacement drug, high blood pressure medications, and a pre-menstrual drug, cough medications containing chloroform (now banned), a drug that treats vaginal infections and an anti-malarial drug. Beware of nitrofurazone, furazolidone, nihydrazone, phenacetin, and duraltadone. No drugs should be taken casually, without strict medical guidance and unless absolutely necessary.

Two drugs need special emphasis. The first is "the Pill," which of course refers to birth control pills for women; and the second is the estrogen pill taken by so many postmenopausal women to put "zest" back into their lives or to keep their skin looking younger. Both pills have now been linked to cancer. Is that any way to treat a body?

"The Pill" fools the body by causing a sort of artificial pregnancy. When this is prolonged, drastic changes can occur that increase the chances of blood clots or cancer.

All of the oral contraceptives use estrogens, which have been shown to cause cancer in humans and animals, at least in higher dosages. Although in wide use for only about fifteen to twenty years, "the Pill" is already linked to increased cervical cancer (especially in those with dysplasia) and liver tumors. Whether or not other cancers will be linked to "the Pill" as years of usage go by and the normal cancer latent period is passed remains to be seen, but already estrogen replacement therapy has been linked to uterine cancer.

Women taking birth control pills need extra amounts of the B-complex vitamins (especially folic acid and B-6), vitamin C, vitamin E and selenium.

Three independent studies have reported an increased risk of endometrial (lining of the uterus) cancer in postmenopausal women taking estrogens for long periods of time.

Vitamin E helps many women through menopause. It reduces hot flashes and emotional problems without the risk of extra estrogens.

Negative or Suppressed Emotions and Attitudes

Dr. Lawrence LeShan, a psychotherapist at the Institute of Applied Biology in New York City, profiled cancer-prone individuals in the early 1950s based on a study of 500 patients.[5] Cancer victims typically suffer from feelings of desertion, loneliness, self-condemnation and guilt, while outwardly projecting a gentle, thoughtful and uncomplaining personality.

Dr. Ronald Grossarth-Maticek of the West German Cancer Research Center in Heidelberg believes the typical cancer victim passively tolerates harmful living or working conditions, tends to put himself down, can't express his innermost feelings and shies away from contact with others. The typical cancer patient also smokes or drinks too much, tends to idealize people around him, likely was misunderstood by his parents and deeply troubled by the loss of a loved one. Dr. Grossarth-Maticek made these conclusions after examining 1,890 patients of which 500 had cancer.[6]

A later study at the University of Rochester Medical Center by Dr. Arthur H. Schmale noted that with few exceptions in 109 patients, the onset of adult leukemia and lymphoma followed a major emotional loss. The study concluded that cancer followed deep feelings of sadness, anxiety, anger or helplessness after the loss of a job or a loved one.[7]

Dr. David Kissen, a Scottish psychologist, on comparing 500 lung cancer patients to 450 persons suffering other serious chest ailments, found that the cancer patients couldn't express their emotions. Dr. Kissen noted that although smoking increased the chances of lung cancer, smoking plus pent-up emotions increased the chances even further.[8]

Dr. Hans Selye, director of the Institute of Experimental Medicine and Surgery at the University of Montreal, concludes that if you have dormant cancer cells and stress paralyzes your body's immune system, cancer will develop.[9]

Dr. Norton F. Kristy, co-director of the Center for Counseling and Psychotherapy in Santa Monica, California, firmly believes that cancer is associated with psychological stress.[10]

In the April 16, 1977 issue of *Lancet,* Australian researchers reported that the white blood cells of bereaved spouses displayed an impaired immunity response to invading agents.

Persons who cope poorly with stress appear to suffer deficits in cell-mediated immunity, according to Dr. Steven Locke of Boston University. Dr. Locke believes that stress alone is not sufficient to impair immunity— the crucial factor is how well a person copes with stress.[11]

Other psychologists believe that cancer patients often are those that "seem to have been alienated from their parents," "are very rigid," "don't get depressed easily and take life as it comes," and "rarely get anxious or angry."

I have noted that those patients "cured" of cancer developed strong wills to live and very positive attitudes. You might as well have a positive attitude now and enjoy life.

Unhappiness seems to deplete nutritional reserves because it keeps taxing the glands to produce hormones related to emotions not normally produced over long periods of time. Happy people seem to live longer and have fewer diseases. Put life in your years and you will add good years to your life.

Geography

There are certain areas in the United States where some cancers are considerably higher than the national average. This is due either to high concentrations of pollutants or to lack of nutrients in the soil, such as the mineral selenium.

Over all the northeast, especially New Jersey, New York, and the coasts of Maine, New Hampshire and Massachusetts, the cancer rate is highest, except for the District of Columbia, in 1978 the highest of all.

Also, the Houston area has a high occurrence of lung and bladder cancer, thought to be due to the high concentration of petrochemical plants there. Lung cancer occurs more often in Washington, D.C. and Baltimore than most other parts of the nation. Cancer of the cervix is highest in Appalachia and the northeastern United States. The southern states have the highest rate of melanoma, an extremely deadly form of skin cancer caused by excess exposure to sunlight. The highest rate of bladder cancer occurs in Salem County, New Jersey, where 25 percent of the men work in chemical plants.

Stomach cancers are higher in the Dakotas, Minnesota, Wisconsin, and Upper Michigan. Breast, colon, rectal, and esophageal cancers are generally more frequent in the north than the south. The northern areas highest in these cancers are New Jersey, southern New York, Connecticut, Rhode Island, Massachusetts, and the cities on the Great Lakes.

In fact, in the 139 counties where the nation's chemical industry is most heavily concentrated, there is much higher than average incidence of bladder, lung and liver cancer. Areas involved in automobile manufacture have high rates of bladder cancer; those areas with chemical industries have high rates of liver and lung cancer; and those with copper and lead smelters have high rates of lung cancer.

The national average cancer death rate is 184 per 100,000 for black males; 174 per 100,000 for white males; 139 per 100,000 for black women, and 130 per 100,000 for white women.

The most cancer-prone cities for white males are:

Baltimore	233	per 100,000
Philadelphia	221	per 100,000
New York	216	per 100,000
Cleveland	212	per 100,000
Detroit	209	per 100,000
Chicago	206	per 100,000
Washington	204	per 100,000
Houston	188	per 100,000
Dallas	178	per 100,000
Los Angeles	175	per 100,000

The highest rates for white females are only slightly different. They are:

New York	160	per 100,000
Baltimore	157	per 100,000
Philadelphia	156	per 100,000
Chicago	149	per 100,000
Cleveland	147	per 100,000
Detroit	143	per 100,000
Washington	142	per 100,000
Los Angeles	132	per 100,000
Houston	124	per 100,000
Dallas	120	per 100,000

For black males, the rates are:

Washington	264	per 100,000

Baltimore	257	per 100,000
Philadelphia	244	per 100,000
New York City	234	per 100,000
Cleveland	229	per 100,000
Chicago	227	per 100,000
Detroit	217	per 100,000
Houston	204	per 100,000
Dallas	188	per 100,000
Los Angeles	186	per 100,000

States with little heavy industry or free of overcrowding and traffic jams are relatively free of cancer. Examples are West Virginia, North Carolina, Arizona, Oklahoma, Kentucky, Utah and New Mexico.

The National Cancer Institute (NCI) has published an *Atlas of Cancer Mortality for U.S. Counties: 1950-1969* showing geographic variation in cancer death rates across the U.S. for thirty-five anatomic sites of cancer.

NCI scientists believe the *Atlas* provides clues to occupational and other environmental factors that contribute to cancer causation. The *Atlas* can be used to identify communities or areas of the U.S. where additional studies may pinpoint these factors.

Authors of the *Atlas* are Thomas J. Mason, Ph.D., Frank W. McKay, Robert Hoover, M.D., William J. Blot, Ph.D., and Joseph F. Fraumeni, Jr., M.D. of NCI's Epidemiology Branch. Modified versions of five of the maps are reproduced here as figures 4.1 to 4.5.

The maps are based on average annual cancer death rates (death per 100,000 population) computed after tabulation of cancer deaths in the U.S. during 1950-1969. This information, obtained from data provided by HEW's National Center for Health Statistics, is based on death certificates.

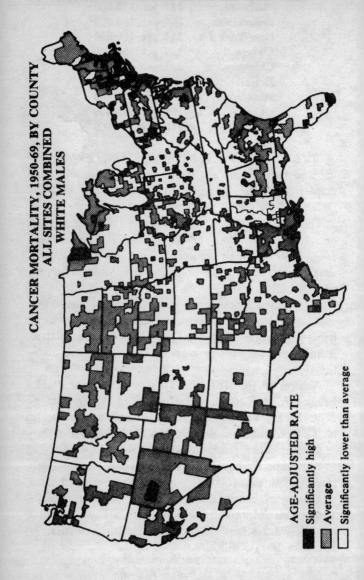

CANCER MORTALITY, 1950-69, BY COUNTY
ALL SITES COMBINED
WHITE MALES

AGE-ADJUSTED RATE

■ Significantly high

▨ Average

□ Significantly lower than average

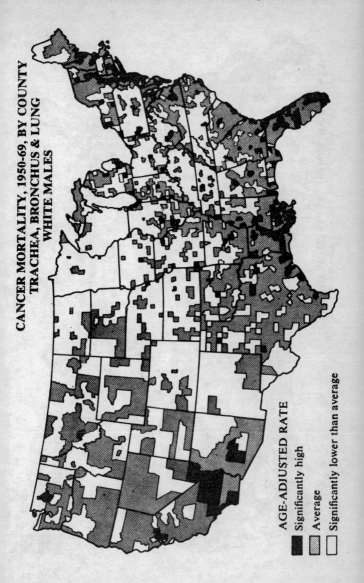

CANCER MORTALITY, 1950-69, BY COUNTY
TRACHEA, BRONCHUS & LUNG
WHITE MALES

AGE-ADJUSTED RATE

Significantly high

Average

Significantly lower than average

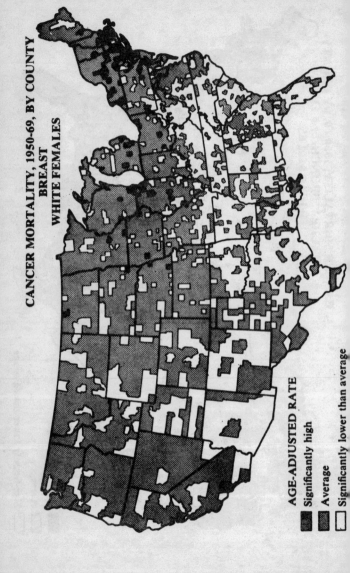

CANCER MORTALITY, 1950-69, BY COUNTY
BREAST
WHITE FEMALES

AGE-ADJUSTED RATE

■ Significantly high

▨ Average

□ Significantly lower than average

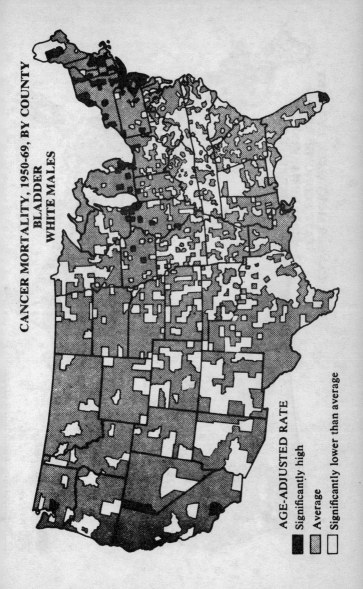

CANCER MORTALITY, 1950-69, BY COUNTY
BLADDER
WHITE MALES

AGE-ADJUSTED RATE

Significantly high

Average

Significantly lower than average

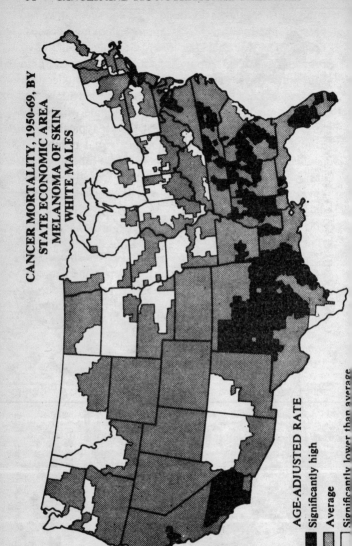

CANCER MORTALITY, 1950-69, BY
STATE ECONOMIC AREA
MELANOMA OF SKIN
WHITE MALES

AGE-ADJUSTED RATE

■ Significantly high

▨ Average

□ Significantly lower than average

So much for the background. You can see that we can prevent much cancer by stopping smoking, occupational safety (or changing jobs), cleaning up the environment and food supply, watching our exposure to sun and X rays, and proper nutrition and moderation in lifestyle. Let's look closely at the role of nutrition.

I have made a very conservative estimate which projects that out of two groups, one group typical of the general population and the other an equal number of people practicing supernutrition, the supernutrition group will have less than 70 percent of the control group's cancer incidence and will have triple its cure rate. This is a bold statement. Of course, it is unproven. What gives me the confidence to make such a statement?

For openers, let me tell you that I make the projection based on animal experiments that anyone can confirm and several researchers have. I take a group of mice, feed them a carcinogen and, depending on the chemical user, a typical experiment can induce stomach or skin cancer in 90 percent of the mice in four months.

Now here's the outstanding news. If I give the mice antioxidant therapy along with the carcinogen, only a few—typically less than 10 percent—will get cancer. And the good news is that the antioxidant therapy consists of such common antioxidant-type of nutrients as vitamin E, vitamin C, vitamin A and selenium. Yes, a person can easily protect himself to a large degree against carcinogen-induced cancers.

Table 4.1
COMMON CARCINOGENS

Chemical Name	Popular Name
Acetamide	
Acetylaminofluorene	2-AAF
Aflatoxin	
Aldrin	
Alpha-naphthylamine	1-NA
Aminodiphenyl	4-ADP
Arsenic dust	
Asbestos	
Auramine	
Benzapyrene	BP
Benzene	
Benzidine	B2D
Benzyl Chloride	
Beta-naphthylamine	2-NA
Beta-propiolactone	BPL
Bis (chloromethyl) ether	BCME
Cadmium dust	
Carbon tetrachloride	
Chloramphenicol	
Chloroethylene	
Chloroform	
Chloromethyl methyl ether	CMME
Chloroporene volatiles	
Coal tar pitch volatiles	
Cyclophosphamide	
Dibenzanthrene	DBA
Dibromochloropropane	DBCP
Dichlorobenzidine	DCB
Dieldrin	
Diethylstilbestrol	DES
Dimethylaminoazobenzene	DAB
Dimethylnitrosamine	DMN
Ethinyl estradiol	
Ethyleneimine	E1

Tris (1, 3-dichloro isopropyl phosphate)	Fyrol
Herbicides	
Melphalan	
Mestranol	
Methyl Methanesulfonate	MMS
Metronidazole	MET
Mustard Gas	
Methylcholanthrene	MCA
Methylene-bis (2-chloroaniline)	MOCA
Methyl Methane Sulfonate	
Naphthylamine	1-NA or 2-NA
Nitrilotriacetic Acid	NTA
Nitrobiphenyl	
Nitrosodimethylamine	DMN
Nitrosopyrrolidine	
Pentachlorophenol	PCP
Pesticides	
Plutonium	
Polychlorinated biphenyls	PCB
Propane Sultone	PS
Propiolactone	BPL
Propylenimine	P1
Tris (2, 3-dibromopropyl phosphate)	Tris
Saccharin	
Safrole	
Sterigmatocystin	
Trichloroethylene	TCE
Urethane	

Table 4.2

HAZARDOUS INDUSTRIES*

Industrial and scientific instruments (solder, asbestos, thallium)

Fabricated metal products (nickel, lead, solvents, chromic acid, asbestos)

Electrical equipment and supplies (lead, mercury, solvents, chlorohydrocarbons, solders)

Machinery except electrical (cutting oils, quench oils, lube oils)

Transportation equipment (constituents of polymers or plastics, including formaldehyde, phenol, isocyanates, amines)

Petroleum and products (benzene, naphthalene, polycyclic aromatics)

Leather products (chrome salts, other organics used in tanning)

Pipeline transportation (petroleum derivatives, metals used in welding)

* From *Science,* September 23, 1977.

References

1. Lyon, Joseph L.; Klauber, Melville R.; Gardner, John W.; and Smart, Charles R. Cancer Incidence in Mormons and Non-Mormons in Utah, 1966-1970. *New England J. Med.*, 294: 3, 129-133, 15 January 1976.

2. Hammond, E. Cuyler. *J. Nat. Cancer Inst.*, 43: 951-962, 1969.

3. Oschner, Alton. *American Scientist*, 59: 246-252, 1971.

4. Hammond, E. Cuyler. *Chemical Engineering News*, Page 4, 5 April 1976.

5. LeShan, Lawrence. *New York Herald Tribune,* 6 April 1965. Also *Cancer Control Journal* 3:5, p. 29, September/October 1975.

6. Grossarth-Maticek, Ronald. *National Enquirer,* 31 May 1977; *Choice,* p. 15, July 1977.

7. Schmale, Arthur H. *New York Herald Tribune,* 6 April, 1965. Also *Cancer Control Journal* 3:5, p. 29, September/October 1975.

8. Kissen, David. *Ibid.*

9. Selye, Hans. *Ibid.*

10. Kristy, Norton. *Ibid.*

11. Locke, Steven. *Science News,* 151, 11 March 1978.

1983 UPDATE

Studies by the Centers for Disease Control of 11,000 women indicate that the "Pill" lowers the overall death rate in women over forty by one-third (*J. Amer. Med. Assoc.* 249, 1591–1596 Feb. 18, 1983). After using the "Pill" for one month, the relative risk of ovarian cancer dropped to six-tenths that of non-users and dropped even lower with further use. Endometrial cancer in Pill users of at least a year dropped to half the risk of non-users.

The statistical increase in breast cancer (1.3 vs 1.0) was attributed to delaying the first pregnancy rather than an effect of the Pill.

Pills having a high ratio of progestin to estrogen alter blood factors in a way that may increase risk of heart attack or stroke (LDL increased, HDL decreased). However Pills having lower progestin-to-estrogen ratios may be protective against heart disease (higher HDL), but their cancer-protecting effect may be lessened (*New Eng. J. Med.,* 308, 862–867, April 14, 1983). Women receiving estrogen injections have four times the risk of breast cancer (*Amer. J. Obstet. Gyn.,* July 1982).

CHAPTER 5

The Winner:
Supernutrition

A 1975 survey of California Mormons showed that they had a cancer death rate and overall death rate only one-half that of the state's overall rate. For six cancer types generally linked to smoking and drinking, the Mormon death rate ranged between 30 to 50 percent of that for the general California death rate. Not surprising, because the moderate lifestyle Mormons are mostly nonsmokers and nondrinkers. So, one could reasonably expect cancers of the lung, esophagus, colon, prostate, kidney, and bladder to be lower in number.

However, Dr. James E. Enstrom, a UCLA epidemiologist, also found that the Mormons had lower rates of cancers of the stomach, rectum, pancreas, breast, uterus and nervous system, as well as lymphomas and leukemia. This is strongly suggestive that moderation in lifestyle and diet are protective against all types of cancer.[1]

Mormons eat well-balanced diets, tend to avoid processed food and junk food, eat ample grains and fruit, and eat meat.

A 1976 study of Utah Mormons by Dr. Joseph L.

Lyon resulted in similar findings. The comparison of Utah Mormons with non-Mormons showed that Mormons had a lower incidence of all cancers associated with smoking, as expected, but again uncovered the unexpected lower incidence of cancers of the breast, uterine cervix, ovary, stomach, and nervous system. Because of the large percentage of Mormons (about 70 percent) in the Utah population, Utah has the least cancer of the 50 states.[2]

Fiber

Colon-rectal cancer is second only to lung cancer in occurrence. Food processing has removed most of the fiber from American diets. Dr. T. L. Cleave, formerly Surgeon-Captain of the Royal British Navy, links cancer, diabetes, heart disease and ulcers together in one—the saccharine disease—caused by the overconsumption of refined carbohydrates.[3]

Dr. Denis P. Burkitt of the British Medical Research Council also believes the high incidence of bowel cancer is largely due to the removal of fiber from the diet. Dr. Burkitt bases his view on his study of people, mostly natives of countries considered less civilized than western nations, who eat high-fiber diets; they are essentially free of this type of cancer.

Dr. Burkitt says, "Many of the diseases of western civilization owe their origin in part to the removal of indigestible fiber from the carbohydrate foods that constitute the major part of our diet."[4]

What we have done is to avoid the complex carbohydrates (starches) and to substitute junk foods made largely of refined sugar and white flour. The milling of flour that makes it "white" throws the germ and high-fiber bran away.

For increased sales appeal, normally pulpy juices are filtered for increased clarity. Solid foods are often separated from fiber, dehydrated, powdered, machine-handled, reconstituted with water to look like the original food, squeezed onto a TV dinner tray, frozen, stored and then heated. No one has worried about the missing fiber because it is indigestible, has no nutrient value and no calories. But it does have its value. Fiber helps keep the bowel healthy by moving food and waste materials along faster, and by holding water.

Americans average about four grams of crude fiber per day; every healthy person should get six to eight grams. If you are eating a highly processed or refined diet, return to natural foods as much as possible. Eat an apple to get pectin, and bran to get cellulose.

One cup of all-bran cereal contains two grams of crude fiber. Three raw carrots or three apples contain as much. Mangoes, turnips, dried beans and peas, and leafy vegetables are other good sources. Some fruit should be eaten every day.

If you can't make these suggested changes, at least add two tablespoons of miller's bran to your cereal or salad. But this is not as effective as eating natural, unprocessed food.

The Hunzakuts are a people said by the World Health Organization to be free from cancer. They eat good foods, eat sparingly, and work hard. Most notably, their diet is rich in vitamin B-17 (Laetrile or amygdalin), selenium, potassium, rubidium and cesium. In the winter, they have little to eat, but do consume several dried apricots, kernels and all, every day. They are removed from pollution and junk foods, as well as from western medicine. Not only are they cancer free, but they claim a large percentage live beyond one hundred years with 130 not uncommon, and a few reaching 150 to 160.

Cancer Patients

So far I have talked about preventing cancer with moderate diets of unprocessed foods. Diet is important to cancer patients as well. What is the value of needed calories and general nutrition to the cancer patient?

Cancer increases the need for calories because it speeds up the basal metabolism rate—the energy produced by food is used more rapidly by the body. Thus cancer patients have to eat more just to maintain their weight.

Cancer also increases the need for protein. Some people believe that one way to "starve" a cancer is to eat a low-protein diet. However, the evidence that I have seen shows that the cancer cells pirate all the protein that they need from other neighboring healthy tissues, if the diet doesn't supply adequate protein. Some researchers call this effect a cancer protein trap, because the cancer commandeers first priority for the dietary protein from the diet and from healthy tissues until the cancer's needs for protein are met. *As the cancer grows, it takes ever-increasing amounts of protein from healthy tissue, which saps the body's strength and ability to function.*

The patient should be less concerned with the size of the tumor and more concerned with the health of the rest of the body. Tumor growth may be cut back or killed by a healthy body's immune system. *Cancer patients usually die from wasting away, not from the size of tumor.*

A second reason that some of the "unorthodox" cancer therapies stress protein-free or low-protein diets is that they are attempting to "save" available pancreatic enzymes for the task of attacking the cancer, rather than being "wasted" in protein metabolism.

If the pancreatic enzyme activity theory does have

validity, then it is important that high quality protein—complete proteins such as egg, milk, soybeans and meat—be eaten to make more pancreatic enzymes. Remember enzymes are primarily protein.

If protein is avoided, there would at first be a saving of the pancreatic enzymes, but then, being unnecessary, they would soon disappear. The body is amazingly efficient; it would not use tissue protein to produce unneeded enzymes. The production of pancreatic enzymes seems to be stimulated by proteins in the diet.

I have not seen evidence that tumors stimulate the production of pancreatic enzymes. I doubt that they do, because the pancreatic enzymes are activated for use by the more alkaline intestines, not by the less alkaline bloodstream.

Dr. Harold Manner of Loyola University of Chicago has seen evidence that the injection of pancreatic enzymes directly into tumors appears to aid in removal of dead tumor tissue.[5]

Perhaps those who have been aided by taking pancreatic enzymes have been aided merely because the digestion of needed protein has been improved, not because enzymes attack cancer.

An unfortunate complication is that cancer—even in early stages—destroys the appetite. Often severe revulsion to food (anorexia) occurs. The lack of nutrition that results prevents the body from maintaining its health to fight the cancer. A high-protein diet, with adequate calories in carbohydrates and fat is indicated. Cancer patients must force themselves to eat well. Good wholesome foods, plenty of supplements and lots of juices are required, anorexia or not. It takes willpower and a will to live.

When the willpower of the patient has been destroyed, loved ones should request hyperalimentation—the parenteral feeding of amino acids, fats, and carbohydrates directly into the arteries or veins.

I am convinced that *supernutrition will improve chances of winning the battle*.

Normally we see patients being "fed" through intravenous feeding by dripping dextrose solution from an elevated container into a vein. This supplies only a limited amount of calories and has questionable merit. Dextrose is a refined sugar. What is needed is food—proteins, fats and carbohydrates. But they can't be injected directly into the small veins like dextrose can and "tube" feeding into the stomach doesn't help if the patient can't absorb the nutrients.

Conventional cancer treatments such as chemotherapy and radiation speed weight loss by destroying nutrients, worsening the appetite loss and causing diarrhea. The vicious cycle must be broken by injecting amino acids, fats and carbohydrates directly into large arteries or veins. A large blood vessel is required to prevent the damage caused by amino acids and fats to small veins. The larger blood vessels provide a greater dilution with blood, so that the nutrients attach themselves to their proper transporters, rather than to vessel walls.

In 1975, a group of Houston researchers headed by Dr. Edward M. Copeland told the Clinical Congress of the American College of Surgeons that hyperalimentation has been successful in replenishing the strength of cancer patients being treated with radiation and chemicals.

Dr. Copeland pointed out, "A malnourished cancer patient is often one whose only hope of cure or relief is treatment which also produces malnutrition. Only a limited amount of malnutrition is tolerated by the human body before death results."[6]

This is the principle of combining nutritional therapy with conventional therapy. I can't help but wonder if perhaps some "nutritional therapies" (avoiding traditional treatment, or using Laetrile) seem to work better at times than radiation or chemotherapy because they nourish rather than add to the fatal malnourishment caused by conventional therapies.

Dr. Stanley J. Dudrick, also of the University of Texas says, "Up until 1972 there was a taboo that said if you fed a cancer patient, you would accelerate the growth of the tumor. We've found that to be untrue."[7]

Dr. Dudrick points out that hyperalimentation was not only useful in treating curable patients, but also in making terminal patients "stronger and more comfortable in their last days."

In the *New York Times*, 25 November, 1977, Jane E. Brody quoted Dr. Dudrick as saying that ten to thirty percent of deaths that occur in hospitals is directly caused by or contributed to by malnutrition.

Dr. Copeland concluded in his report, "Intravenous nutritional replenishment can convert the weakly reactive patient into an adequately nourished, strongly reactive patient." He also believes that the well-nourished patient's immune system is more likely to efficiently recognize and destroy the cancer cells.

Remember that protein is necessary to make the enzyme that the body needs to destroy the cancer.

Dr. E. Cheraskin and his group at the University of Alabama have shown that those patients given greater amounts of animal protein, multivitamins and minerals, vitamin C and bioflavonoid supplementation, and who eliminated the consumption of refined carbohydrates, had significantly better response to radiation therapy than matched controls. Thus they were expected to have a better survival rate.[8]

Dr. Cheraskin was questioned about this experiment by reporter Jacqueline Himelstein. He elaborated on his published paper. "Just one week of supernutrition prior to radiation therapy for cancer dramatically improves a patient's chance of recovery. In our experiment, only 59 percent of the patients not on the diet were found to have better than 70 percent of their cancer cells destroyed. But in the group on the super-nutrition diet, 100 percent of the patients—every single one of them—had a favorable response. All of them were found to have had more than 90 percent of their cancer cells destroyed by the radiation treatment."[9]

Dr. Dean Burk, retired from the National Cancer Institute after thirty-five years of cancer research, commented on the experiment conducted by Dr. Cheraskin's group. "A high carbohydrate diet would be harmful for people suffering from cancer, since cancer cells flourish on glucose in the system. It's a mystery to me why there has not been follow-up research on his study."[10]

Further support for the value of proper nutrition is given by Dr. Giovanni Costa of the State University of New York at Buffalo, who was quoted by reporter Maury Breecher in the *National Enquirer* on 7 February 1978. "Nutritional support, along with cancer therapy, can extend survival time from six months to five years depending on the type of cancer. Cancer patients lose proteins and calories. When you are under-fed, all of your bodily defenses are gone. You cannot develop antibodies. *But with proper proteins, calories, vitamins and trace minerals, your antibodies come back.*" (Emphasis added.)

Dr. Gio Gori of the National Cancer Institute added, "Some cancer patients actually starve to death. They don't eat enough and they waste away. They lose their ability to cope with infection. A better-fed patient is more likely to withstand the oppressive therapy we give today, but nutritional support is not being used very extensively. In some cases, the cancer therapy itself creates problems by damaging or destroying portions of the digestive system."

Breecher's article also mentioned that Dr. George Blackburn of the Harvard Medical School said, "There are certain types and stages of cancer where *proper nutrition will extend quality and longevity of a patient's life by 50 percent.*" (Emphasis added.)

There is a lot of debate on the low-protein, high-protein diet. Both sides raise interesting points. Why isn't more research being done on this issue?

Calories

I made a big point of cancer patients needing extra calories because their metabolism is increased. They have to fight just to maintain weight.

However, to reduce one's risk of getting cancer in the first place, watch your calories. Animal experiments have shown that extra calories increase the incidence of tumors and shorten the time in which they develop. This may have to do with body fat being a rich source of free radicals.

The incidence of every type of tumor is greater in heavy rats than in lean rats. Epidemiological studies have shown that obesity is significantly related to cancers of the breast, endometrium and gallbladder.[11]

There is also some evidence suggesting that cancer of the uterus occurs more frequently in overweight women.[12] Insurance records show that obese policy holders have a higher cancer death rate.

Meats and Fats

We have heard much from a few researchers about meats, cholesterol and saturated fats causing cancer. There is no relationship. However, too much polyunsaturated fat and too many calories can cause or contribute to cancer.

Meat was suspect when many researchers thought cancer was caused by viruses. Meats release ammonia, which makes cells more susceptible to viral attack. The

Mormon studies absolve meats. Researchers have tried to link saturated fat, cholesterol and meat to changes in the bacteria that normally inhabit the intestine. The change in bacteria pattern would increase the release of chemicals that cause or aid cancer development, in their view. Meat diets encourage *E Coli* bacteria, whereas milk and vegetables encourage *L Acidophilus* bacteria. I have closely watched researchers investigate this avenue of research at the Frederick Cancer Research Center of the National Cancer Institute for five years, with nary a confirmation of this theory. If you want to be sure, take extra *Lactobacillus Acidophilus,* which is available from health food stores or drug stores.

On the other hand, my own experiments, as well as those of many other researchers, have shown that the excessive amount of free radicals released by eating more polyunsaturated fatty acid than the body can handle will increase the probability of getting cancer.[13]

Besides the free radicals produced in polyunsaturated fats, a chemical, malonaldehyde, is formed when the polyunsaturated fats turn rancid. Dr. Raymond J. Shamberger and Charles E. Willis of the Cleveland Clinic have done interesting research on malonaldehyde as a cause of cancer, and on vitamin E and selenium as protectors against the formation of malonaldehyde-induced cancer.[14]

Another carcinogen, methylcholanthrene, can be formed when the fat of meat is heated to very high temperature. Methylcholanthrene not only can cause cancer itself, but even trace quantities can sensitize the body so that other carcinogens start cancer at lower concentrations.

A quarter pound of charcoal-broiled steak contains as much of the carcinogen benzopyrene as the smoke of two packs of cigarettes. Inhaling benzopyrene is far more deadly than eating it, but mice fed benzopyrene develop stomach or bone cancer, or even leukemia.

Don't be misled into thinking that you need more polyunsaturated fats to prevent heart disease. Polyunsaturated fatty acids lower neither the incidence nor death rate of heart disease; a detailed explanation of this can be found in the first eight chapters of my book, *Supernutrition for Healthy Hearts* (Dial Press, 1977, Jove, 1978).

Also, keep in mind the Mormon study: the meat-eating Mormans had less cancer (including colon-rectal cancers) than vegetarian Seventh-day Adventists.

References

1. Enstrom, James E. and Austin, Donald F. *Science,* 4 March 1977.

2. Lyon, Joseph L. *New England J. Med.* 294: 3, 129-133, 15 January 1976.

3. Cleave, T. L. *The Saccharine Disease.* New Canaan, Connecticut: Keats Publishing, 1975.

4. Burkitt, Denis P. *Br. Med. J.* 1:274-78, 1973.

5. Manner, Harold. Natural Health Federation Conference. Chicago, September 1977. Also: *Choice,* September 1977.

6. Copeland, Edward M. Report given at the Clinical Congress of the American College of Surgeons, San Francisco, 14 October 1975.

7. Dudrick, Stanley J. Comments at the Clinical Congress of the American College of Surgeons, 14 October 1975.

8. Cheraskin, E. et al. *Acta Cytologica,* 12:6 433-438, 1968.

9. Himelstein, Jacqueline. AP press release after American College of Surgeons meeting, 14 October 1975.

10. Burk, Dean. *Ibid.*

11. Wynder, E. and Mabuch, K. *Preventive Medicine,* 1:300, 1972. de Waard, F. Key Biscayne Conference, May 1975.

12. Goodhart, Robert S. and Shils, Maurice. *Modern Nutrition in Health and Disease: Dietotherapy.* Philadelphia: Lea and Febiger, 1973.

13. Ackerman, L. V. *Nutr. Today*, 7:2, 1972. Bjork-sten, J. *Science*, 175:474, 1971. Harman, D. *Lancet*, 2:1116, 1957. —— *J. Gerontology*, 26:451, 1971. Knet, J. and Mahboubi, E. *Science*, 175:846, 1972. Kummerow, F. A. *Symposium on Foods: Lipids and Their Oxidation*. Westport, Connecticut: Avi Publishing Co., 1962. Pass-water, R. A. *Amer. Lab.* 5:6 10-22, 1973, Pearce, M. L. and Dayton, S. *Lancet*, 2:464, 1971. Pinckney, E. R. *The Cholesterol Controversy*. Los Angeles, California: Sherbourne Press, 1973. —— *Med. Counterpoint*. Racker, E. *Amer. J. Med.*, 35:143, 1963. *Modern Nutrition in Health and Disease*. Subbiah, M. T. R. *Mayo Clinic. Proc.* 46:549, 1971. Tappel, A. L. *Pathological Aspects of Cell Membranes*. New York: Academic Press, 1971. West, C. E. and Redgrave, T. G. *Amer. Lab.*, 23-30, January 1975. (*Also see* Notes 6-10 in References for chapter Ten.)

14. Shamberger, Raymond J. and Willis, Charles E. *J. Nat. Cancer Inst.*, 48:5, 1491-1497, 1972.

1983 UPDATE

Studies continue to support the concept that cancer patients need more calories than they tend to want, and, that healthy people desiring to prevent cancer do better on fewer calories than they often want.

The cancer patient should consult "How to Nourish the Cancer Patient" by Dr. Maurice Shils (*Nutr. Today* 4–16, May/June 1981) and "Practical Hints for Feeding the Cancer Patient" by Dr. Abby Bloch (*Nutr. Today* 23–25 Nov./Dec. 1981).

Those interested in prevention should consult the National Academy of Sciences' Expert Panel on Cancer publication, "Diet, Nutrition, and Cancer" (*Nat. Acad. Press* 1982). This report stresses controlling *total* fats to 30–35 percent of diet calories (or even a little less) and adding more vegetables to the standard diet. Good advice.

It should also be noted that the more recent studies of the Hunzakuts find that they are neither cancer-free or as long lived as previously claimed. The earlier concept was due to poor data confirmation procedures.

CHAPTER 6

Additives and "Safety"

THE nutritive value of food is important to the good health needed to destroy or ward off cancer. However, food must be examined not only for its nutrients, but also for pollutants—such as additives and pesticides—that cause cancer.

The Delaney Clause was meant to protect us from cancer-causing chemicals in our food. What is the Delaney Clause? Has it become outdated, as some scientists claim?

Most of the additives tested for safety in our food supply are tried out on laboratory animals such as rodents. Are rodents relevant to humans? Nearly everyone laughed when the Canadian tests of saccharin revealed that the equivalent amount of saccharin required in humans to simulate the rat cancer test would be 800 12-ounce diet sodas daily. Is that a meaningful test?

What would happen to us and our children if our testing procedures were changed or the Delaney Clause weakened? Should food be considered on the same benefit/risk ratio as drugs?

The need to protect people by regulating what industry can put into food was recognized by Congress early in this century. The Pure Food Act of 1906 was enacted, largely due to the lobbying efforts of Dr. H. W. Wiley, who was then made first commissioner of the Food and Drug Administration.

However, Dr. Wiley became disillusioned by industry's efforts to bypass the simple measures taken then to protect our health. Dr. Wiley's 1912 letter of resignation stated in part: "I saw the fundamental principles of the Food and Drug Act . . . one by one paralyzed or discredited. Interest after interest engaged in . . . the manufacture of misbranded or adulterated foods and drugs. . . . One by one, I found [my] activities were restricted. . . . A few of the instances of this kind are well known. Among these may be mentioned the . . . addition to food of benzoic acid . . . of saccharin . . . the selling of moldy, fermented, decomposed and misbranded grains."

In 1958, the Food and Drug Act of 1938 was considerably strengthened by a Food Additive amendment authored by Representative James J. Delaney (Dem., N.Y.) which requires that any food additive found carcinogenic in man or animal be banned from food consumed in the United States. The food industry seems to have been trying to weaken or get rid of the Delaney Clause ever since.

The exact wording of the clause is important. It prohibits approval of a food *additive* "If a fair evaluation of the data before the Secretary . . . fails to establish that the proposed use of the food additive, under the conditions of use to be specified in the regulation will be safe . . ." No food additive "shall be deemed to be safe if it is found, *after tests which are appropriate* for the evaluation of the safety of food additives, to induce cancer in man or animal." [Emphasis added.]

Several scientists feel that the Delaney Clause is impractical, that potentially beneficial chemicals are being banned when, if used in low levels, they would be safe. They feel that the clause is an absolutist approach that only considers risks without benefits.

Other scientists feel that there is no need to have any risk added to food, that we should stay on the safe side because we do not have adequate means of projecting unforeseen risks wherein one compound may potentiate another. They feel that there is no need for food coloring (except to hide defects) or color-preserving nitrites and nitrates (except to hide age) in today's world of refrigeration.

Dr. Frederick Coulston of Albany Medical College says, "I would like to see the Delaney Clause repealed entirely." Dr. Coulston feels that tolerance levels can be set for chemical carcinogens. "There is a time-dose response for every chemical, and every chemical also has a no-effect level—even cyanide." This principle is widely recognized and used in setting radiation limits and pesticide residue limits.

Dr. Coulston summarizes his views: "Concerning the Delaney Clause, one can state unequivocally that there is nothing wrong with its intent and philosophy. No one wants to put a hazardous chemical that may be a carcinogen into our food. . . . Therefore, in spite of the implied risk, I advocate that even a potential chemical carcinogen could be used in food—allowing for a safety factor in its dose level—if on balance the substance is beneficial to man."[1]

Other scientists point out that Canada and European countries allow reasonable limits to be set rather than complete banning of the additives. They wonder what happens as our analytical techniques for detecting traces of pollutants become so sensitive, that airborne contamination during normal raising of crops, would technically prohibit the sale of those crops under the Delaney Clause.

The other side of the debate also has interesting questions. Dr. Sidney M. Wolfe of the Health Research Group says, "Food additives are largely of benefit to industry—hustling the sale of billions of artificial products that appear to taste, smell, feel, and look like something they are not. In passing the Delaney Clause, Congress said, in essence, that no benefit to consumers of any food additive can be so great that it outweighs the risk, however small, of cancer to the large proportion of the population using food additives."

Dr. Wolfe remarks, "Objections to the Delaney Clause have to do with so-called trace amounts of chemicals, which were previously undetectable and which now exist only because of advances in instrumentation. There are two major reasons why this objection—like the benefit and animal irrelevance objections—is itself irrelevant. The overwhelming majority of food additives are not present in trace amounts. Indeed, flavors, colors, emulsifiers, and other additives often reach levels of hundreds of parts per million or more."[2]

Dr. Wolfe contends that although it is theoretically possible that there is a dose or exposure level of a carcinogenic food additive below which none of the 200 million Americans who use it regularly will get cancer, in practice there is no way to determine what this "safe" threshold is.

But keep in mind that not everyone agrees with the radiation standards. Damage inflicted by radiation appears to be proportional to the amount of radiation, even at the lowest levels measured. The incidence of lung cancer appears to be proportional to the number of cigarettes smoked.

As an example of variation in human sensitivity, the FDA has estimated that if everyone drank 800 cans of saccharin-sweetened soda a day and were as sensitive to its cancer-causing properties as the Canadian male rats, there would be about forty million cases of bladder cancer. If everyone drank *only one* can of such soda a day over a lifetime, this could produce as many as 1200 cases of bladder cancer a year.

Suppose humans were more sensitive than rats.

The Delaney Clause does not apply to environmental contaminants and natural carcinogens such as aflatoxin, so the concern about airborne contaminants is needless. Unfortunately, the Delaney Clause does not apply to chemicals that are safe in themselves, but react in the body to form carcinogens (such as nitrates forming nitrosamines), nor does it apply to chemicals that cause birth defects.

Can Animal Tests Determine Safety?

Dr. John O. Nestor of the FDA commented on the Delaney Clause in the spring of 1977:

"In my opinion, the following points demonstrate that the Delaney Amendment is both good science and good law:

"(1) A large percentage of cancers now developing in our population are due directly or indirectly to extrinsic factors such as food additives, chemicals, radiation, viral infections, etc.

"(2) At present, there is no known minimal or threshold dose below which a carcinogen can be considered safe.

"(3) Our present bioassays (animal experiments) involving only a limited number of animals (a few hundred at the most) are insensitive. Thus, when positive, they indicate the substance being tested is a strong carcinogen. To detect weak carcinogens requires testing thousands of animals. Accordingly, we must pay great attention to the warning signal represented by a positive animal test.

"(4) Practically without exception, substances that have been found to be carcinogenic in man have also proven to be carcinogenic in animals. We must assume that any substance which is carcinogenic in animals could also be so in man. We cannot wait for the outcome of lengthy and complex epidemiological studies in man. . . ."[3]

In Canada, it is true that they don't have a specific Delaney-type of carcinogen clause. The Canadian law simply states, "No person shall sell an article of food that has in or upon it any poisonous or harmful substance." As one Canadian government official was quoted, "We don't know that much about cancer, how it is produced . . . therefore, we can't be sure what is a safe level."[4]

Dr. William Lijinsky of the Frederick Cancer Research Center says, "There is no way of establishing a safe threshold dose of a carcinogen. Even though one might agree that there must be a no-effect level, we do not know how to determine what that is."[5]

Dr. Donald Kennedy, in his first press conference as FDA Commissioner (April 1977), explained:

"The exposure of test animals to high doses is the most valid way we know to predict whether a chemical may cause cancer in people. Such tests are both realistic and reliable.

"They are, in fact, essential to predict rare occurrences—for example, to seek out and identify a substance that can cause cancer in only one out of every 20,000 Americans. That may be a rare occurrence statistically but it's still more than 10,000 people in our population.

"It is essential that we use test animals to help us identify, early enough to do something about them, the suspicious chemicals to which we may be exposed in the foods we eat, the drugs we use, the water we drink, and the air we breathe.

"It's fairly easy for reasonable people to understand why we must use animals to try to predict which chemicals will and which will not be likely to hurt people. It is harder to understand why science must test these animals with doses far larger than humans are ever likely to receive. The first answer is practicality.

"No one could breed, raise, sacrifice and examine test animals fast enough to find one case of cancer out of 20,000 animals. There aren't enough breeders, examiners, time, or money.

"Instead, we use fewer animals. And to compensate for that, we use high doses. And over the years we have established that the system works! Animal tests identical in principle to those used for saccharin have demonstrated cancer in animals for virtually all the chemicals known to cause cancer in people.

"So, if a chemical tested in high doses on a limited number of animals causes cancer, we are concerned. We are concerned for two reasons: First, because science warns us that if a high dose of something causes cancer in a significant number of test animals, a low dose may cause cancer in some people; and, second, science reassures us that most chemicals do *not* cause cancer no matter how high the dose. It's simply not true, as many people believe, that too much of almost anything will cause cancer.

"In fact, in 1969, the National Cancer Institute reported that of 120 pesticides and industrial compounds given to mice, only eleven were found definitely to induce tumors. And these chemicals were not randomly selected. Most were picked because there already was reason to suspect that they might cause cancer. Even so, the great majority of more than 100 suspicious chemicals did not cause cancer in animals when tested at high dose levels.

". . . From animal studies we can estimate that the risk of bladder cancer in humans may be increased by only 0.04 percent by saccharin. To measure such a small statistical increase in human risk would require the study of not thousands, but tens of thousands of people, and not for two to four years, but for decades. We simply can't wait that long.

". . . With a thousand Americans a day already dying from cancer, with another 1,600 new cases being detected daily, and with the knowledge that we don't know what causes most of these cancers, then I think that we as a nation cannot ignore the kind of evidence that we now have against saccharin."

The Canadian saccharin tests used 100 rats, which received 5 percent of their diet as saccharin. Only 8.9 percent of the rats developed tumors. A tenfold reduction in dose should produce a tenfold reduction in tumor frequency. Therefore, less than one rat in the hundred tested would develop cancer, an effect impossible to detect.

Epidemiological studies have only been able to discern differences greater than 30 percent in cancer incidences.

Natural variability among people is another reason to test at high-dose levels. Laboratory animals respond much more uniformly to carcinogens because they are highly inbred. High doses help balance animal studies in favor of those people most susceptible.

As you see there is individuality in response to cancer-causing chemicals. Part of the individuality is due to genetics and part is due to nutrition. I believe there is evidence that well-nourished individuals can tolerate larger doses of carcinogens.

Critics of the large-dose experiments in animals rationalize that at these high doses, the crystals of saccharin may precipitate in the bladder, irritating the bladder wall, which in turn could cause tumors.

A shaky scheme of "ifs." No one has reported finding such crystals or irritations. On the other hand, three of the major industrial human carcinogens (estrogens, bis-chloromethyl ether and vinyl chloride) were all determined to be carcinogenic in animal experiments.

A word should be said about probability. If a chemical fails to produce cancer in a group of 100 mice, this merely means that at the 99 percent confidence level, it is likely to produce cancer in less than 5 percent of the test animals. Five percent of the American population is 10 million people. By the laws of statistics and logic, the margin of error is such that the compound may be safe or could cause up to 10 million Americans to develop cancer.

The same statistics applied to the United States population would indicate that there is 99 percent certainty that the chemical that produces no detectable cancer in 100 mice will produce cancer in less than ten million Americans.

Remember, cancer can easily be missed in animals because it's hard to detect in its early stages. A substantial portion of an animal's lifetime is required to allow the cancer to develop. How many have been missed?

The Delaney Clause is a valuable weapon. Just having it in view prevents a lot of trouble. Can you imagine what industry would try if there were no Delaney Clause?

Let Them Eat Additives

There are 3,000 additives now in use. At best their effects are themselves mathematically additive, and at worst synergistic.

As Nicholas Von Hoffman has said, "To be safe, additives don't need to be tested but banished from the food chain. And don't believe the scare talk that it would make food either more expensive or harder to get. The only difference is that industrially processed near food—such as Hofflefinger's Banana Yellow Yum-Yums—would vanish and maraschino cherries would no longer glow in the dark."[6]

"The average American eats about nine pounds of *unnecessary* food additives a year—and nobody knows how many of them are," says Dr. James Thomson of the University of Surrey in Guildford, England. He says only half of the 3,000 additives in use are useful; the others are only cosmetic to make something appear as it is not.

Dr. Thomson also points out, "Many additives have not been tested for safety, and even those which have been tested and found harmless may well be dangerous when mixed with other additives. Nobody knows how dangerous the unneeded cosmetic food additives are in the long run, and they should be cut out of food altogether."[7]

Government figures show a rapid growth in additive usage—both in number of new additives and quantity of usage. In 1966, our average annual additive intake was 3 pounds; in 1971, it was 4 pounds; in 1974, it was 5 pounds, and in 1977, it was 9 pounds.

Industry reports project increasing growth in the 1980s. In 1974, additive sales were 853 million dollars, in 1975, sales were 936 million dollars, and projections for 1984 (constant dollars) exceed 1.3 billion dollars. The industrial output of synthetic organic chemicals has leaped from 15 billion pounds in 1945 to over 167 billion pounds in 1972.

Aside from food additives, a preliminary EPA survey suggests that there are between 70,000 and 100,000 known chemicals, as well as an additional 1,000 new ones coming on the market each year.

At the present time, the EPA has only 100 people working on toxic chemicals; even if they had 4,000 people, they couldn't do a good job on detecting and testing 70,000 chemicals for their toxicity.

The FDA has started a review of those additives generally recognized as safe (GRAS). The GRAS list is made up of hundreds of food additives. (It's hard to believe that they can examine more than twenty a year.) What do we do in the meantime? We can avoid or cut back our usage of the most suspicious. The following chapter discusses the most obvious dangers.

References

1. Coulston, Frederick. *Chemical & Engineering News*, p. 34, 27 June 1977.

2. Wolfe, Sidney M. *Ibid.*, p. 38.

3. Nestor, John O. *Washington Star*, 19 March 1977.

4. *National Health Federation Bulletin*, June 1977.

5. Lijinsky, William. *Chemical & Engineering News*, p. 24, 27 June 1977.

6. Hoffman, Nicholas von. *Playboy*, March 1977.

7. Thomson, James. UPI story in the *Los Angeles Times*, p. 32, 18 January 1977.

1983 UPDATE

A report by the Office of Technology Assessment found that data that chemical manufacturers provide the Environmental Protection Agency on new compounds is lacking toxicity data in almost half (47 percent) of the reports sent to the agency. Only 17 percent included any data for chronic (long-term) toxicity and this was usually a simple mutagenicity test (*Chem. Eng. News* 34, May 2, 1983).

Not every compound causes cancer. Of 7,000 compounds tested, 6,500 were found to be safe. Some compounds that do cause cancer will not even be encountered by the average person. Still we must keep our guard up and insist that everything is suspect until proven otherwise.

CHAPTER 7

Known Food Hazards

IT is folly to classify items into a category for one purpose and then assume that all items in that category automatically are similar in all respects. In other words, all additives are not necessarily harmful just because they are additives.

Some additives may be very beneficial to us. However, I haven't seen sufficient evidence to allow me to positively identify a "good" additive yet. Salt enhances the flavor of some foods, but elevates blood pressure in many people. Sugar sweetens nicely, but it is overused and adds too many empty calories, makes "plastic" foods acceptable to taste, which dilutes the nutritive value of the diet, and it is a problem to diabetics and hypoglycemics.

Even some of the synthetic chemicals may be a benefit to us. For example, I have done many experiments that show butylated hydroxytoluene (BHT) reduces cancer incidence and lengthens the average and maximum lifespans of mice. Since BHT has come into wide usage, stomach cancer has declined, probably because we eat less rancid food which is rich in cancer-causing free radicals.

Yet I don't know if BHT is safe to use in man, and I am concerned that BHT is in nearly every packaged food you pick up. In my lab, I saw nothing but good effects from BHT. I did notice that my mice were more active, but this was because epinephrine (adrenalin) levels were slightly increased and they required less sleep. Some of the male mice seemed to be more aggressive, but I noticed this effect with large amounts of vitamin E also. I have carried nearly one thousand mice through four generations of BHT use without observing any abnormalities.

Still this doesn't preclude the possibility that they were there. For example, a report from England associates blindness with BHT. I never once deliberately examined my mice for blindness. They seemed symptom-free, but I can't certify that some of the mice weren't blind.

Another English report associates liver tumors with BHT at extremely high dosage. I found at my low doses, that BHT prevented the cancers that normally develop when the mice were given certain known chemical carcinogens.

We do know that some people are seriously allergic to this compound. Could it also cause behavioral problems, birth defects and cancer in certain susceptible individuals?

See how important it is to do lots of tests at several doses with many animals, even different species?

Should BHT be in widespread use without further testing? It is a preservative. Vitamin E is a natural preservative. Would we be better off if vitamin E were added to the oil-containing foods in which BHT is now used?

Camouflage

If an additive is used for deception, it clearly presents a

double risk. First, the effect that it is covering up presents risk; second, the unneeded chemical itself is a risk.

Adding dark coloring to "enriched" white bread to make it look like whole wheat bread is a dark deception indeed. Surely it is adulteration to use caramel coloring to make breads look like the darker and more nutritious whole-grain breads. Yellow coloring is often used to imitate the presence of butter or egg.

Nearly four million dollars worth (1.3 million pounds) of Amaranth (Red Dye No. 2), a certified food coloring until 1976, was used to entice or mislead people into buying 10 billion dollars worth of food products yearly. Red Dye No. 2 was in so many things—not just red foods. It made white cake icing look whiter and chocolate look browner. It was in red, orange, and purple colored "products" as well. Cherry, grape, cream, root beer, and strawberry soft drinks contained it. It was in gelatins, puddings, jams, jellies, preserves, yogurts, fruit juices, cakes, cookies, cocoa, candies, ice cream, soups, cereals, dog foods, maraschino cherries, cough medicines, vitamin pills, cosmetics, and—well, in fact, nobody has a complete list of what products contained the dye because dyes or coloring do not have to be listed on labels. Shouldn't that be changed?

The dye was never found to be safe, but the FDA allowed it on a provisional basis since 1960—while the manufacturers stalled on the safety tests—until 1976 when other new tests found it to be a carcinogen. The dye industry responded not by helping, but by trying to block the FDA ban—all the way to Chief Justice Warren E. Burger—to overturn the ban while they appealed the ruling in the lower court.

Consumers and the health food industry had been trying to get rid of Red Dye No. 2 for many years. Other countries had banned it, and nine other tests had shown it to cause cancer, birth defects and miscarriages in animal experiments. Finally, the General Accounting Office (GAO) got after the FDA in October 1975 for postponing a decision on the safety of the dye fourteen times since 1963 at the request of the food and cosmetic industry, even though there often was no indication that evidence determining its safety would be forthcoming. The GAO report to Senator Gaylord Nelson (D. Wisc.) finally pushed the FDA into action.

The FDA issued its ban on Red Dye No. 2 in January 1976, and nearly every food processor switched to Red Dye No. 40. But by the end of the following month, the FDA issued the following press release:

> The Food and Drug Administration is evaluating new information which raises questions about the safety of Red No. 40, an artificial color used in foods, drugs, and cosmetics.
>
> The new data were presented to the Agency February 25, 1976, by Allied Chemical, which holds the patent on Red No. 40. The data show that after 41 weeks of a 78-week feeding study involving 400 mice, six of the animals had developed premature and unexpected malignant lymphomas. FDA asked Allied to move as quickly as possible to sacrifice additional mice from the study to determine the significance of these highly preliminary findings. The work will require a minimum of 30 days.
>
> The study is being conducted for Allied by Hazleton Laboratories of Vienna, Virginia.
>
> The Agency cautioned that no conclusions about the safety of Red No. 40 could be reached on the basis of the interim report.
>
> FDA intends to present all available data on Red No. 40 to its Toxicology Advisory Committee March 8 and 9, 1976.
>
> Allied undertook the study at the request of the World Health Organization, the Food and Agriculture Organization, and the Canadian government, which has not approved Red No. 40 for use in that country.
>
> The FDA evaluation of Red No. 40 is part of the

Agency's continuing review of all artificial food colors now approved or provisionally listed by the Agency for use in U.S. products.

In January, 1976, the Agency ordered Red No. 2 off the market, pending better evidence of safety for human use. Red No. 40 rapidly is being adopted by industry as the principal alternative to Red No. 2.

(A preliminary report issued in May 1978 indicates that Red No. 40 may be safe, but further tests were planned.)

Previously the dye Violet No. 1 was banned after studies showed it to cause cancer. It had been in use for twenty years.

Is it really necessary that our food be bright red, orange, purple, white or brown? What's wrong with food's real colors? If we must add color, can't natural colorings be used? When the public switches, so will the profit-minded manufacturers.

Nitrite

Nitrates and nitrites don't cause cancer. However, in the body, nitrite (and nitrate which is converted to nitrite in the stomach) combines with certain amines to form nitrosamines, which do cause cancer. But nitrates and nitrites escape the Delaney Clause because they themselves are not direct causes.

Nitrates and nitrites are saltlike chemicals added to meats to guard against botulism and preserve color (deception?) and flavor.

More nitrite is used than is needed to prevent botulism; and since most processed meats are kept refrigerated and botulism can be destroyed in cooking, I suspect the overusage of nitrite is merely to keep the meat fresher looking longer.

Dr. Donald Houston, assistant deputy director of the United States Department of Agriculture, said in October, 1975, "The use of nitrite as a curing agent in meats should be limited because cooking nitrite-cured bacon produces substances that cause cancer in rats. The nitrite-cured bacon produces low levels of nitrosamines—between 5 to 15 parts per billion—when cooked at high temperatures."

Dr. Houston added, "If you reduce the level of cooking to the point at which nitrosamines are not produced, you have the problem of botulism. What we are trying to do is lower the levels of nitrite in bacon so cooking doesn't produce nitrosamines and at the same time, maintain enough levels to prevent danger from botulism. *We know* the present levels *aren't necessary,* so we are cutting back."[1]

We now know that the nitrosamines can form in the stomach from nitrites and amines normally present. So the danger isn't limited to cooking. We have also learned that vitamin C can block the formation of the cancer-causing nitrosamines in the stomach and during cooking. The chapter on vitamin C will discuss how this danger can be controlled either by adding vitamin C to processed meats or taking vitamin C supplements.

At the same time, the amount of nitrates and nitrites in meats should be lowered. Dr. R. F. Kelly of the Department of Food Science and Technology at Virginia Polytechnic Institute comments, "Sometimes we have to change our minds about what is good. Today, many meat products do not taste as they used to; many of our ideas about color also have changed. Once upon a time, I thought we could use antibiotics to reduce spoilage of country hams. All my ideas on this have changed—slowly, but surely. The point is, we can, *if we have to,* change our processing techniques to accommodate the new rules of the game. Can we produce meat products without the use of nitrates or nitrites? My answer is, Yes."[2]

Dr. Kelly went on to describe many techniques that

might even improve the quality and taste of meat—safely, without nitrates or nitrites.

DES

In twenty years the Delaney Clause has been invoked only eight times. DES in animal feeds was one of them, but there still seems to be DES occasionally in beef livers, because the ban was modified to allow DES to be used in feed, as long as it is discontinued fourteen days prior to slaughter so that no residues are found in the carcass or liver.

DES is the synthetic sex hormone, diethylstilbestrol. Animals given DES grow bigger and faster on the same amount of feed. This extra growth produces enough extra meat for a given amount of feed to lower beef production costs by about three cents a pound. One wonders if the risk from a proven carcinogen is worth the saving of three cents a pound.

DES was used thirty years ago to prevent miscarriage during the first three months of pregnancy. However, the daughters of these women developed reproductive system abnormalities twenty to thirty years later.

The FDA has tried various techniques since the late 1950s to prevent the use of DES, and Congress has weighed several measures to prevent the use of DES in all but emergency cases as a morning-after contraceptive.

DES was first added to cattle feed in 1954. The FDA banned its use from 1958 to 1962, but cattle industry legal maneuvers led to a compromise that DES could be used as long as no residues be detected in meat. In the early 1970s the U.S. Department of Agriculture meat inspection program uncovered increasing DES residue levels and occurrences. The FDA tightened up on its regulation, but during 1974, seven violations out of 3,050 samples showed significant DES levels.

The FDA banned DES, but the courts overturned the FDA action because the FDA failed to hold proper hearings. During 1975 and 1976, the USDA said DES levels were as high as they were during 1972, the peak years of abuse. As of early 1978, DES is still allowed in animal feeds, on the condition it be discontinued fourteen days prior to slaughter.

If DES is finally banned in feed, some cattlemen will use ear implants of DES to circumvent the ban. As long as DES is not detected in the meat, the FDA seems to be powerless to act on druglike usage in the animals. Perhaps we need more sensitive detection procedures to reduce the allowable DES levels.

Pesticides and Fungicides

During June 1975, Japan rejected more than 255,000 cartons of American lemons, oranges, and grapefruits because they contained two fungicides (OPP and TBZ) acceptable to Americans, but banned by Japan. The Japanese were so worried they wouldn't allow the spoiling fruit to be dumped in the ocean for fear of contaminating their waters. Yet Americans eat these chemicals!

In 1974, the Environmental Protection Agency had overwhelming evidence that the pesticides Aldrin and Dieldrin caused cancer. In spite of their estimates that continued use at the 1975 rate for another year to year and a half would cause 230,000 cases of cancer, they were prevented (at that time) from banning the pesticides.

The EPA also withdrew its case against the pesticide 2,4,5-T in 1974, stating the evidence against it was insufficient. DDT is harmless by comparison. Be sure to wash foods that may have pesticides on them.

Pentachlorophenol (PCP) is a carcinogen in so many foods, such as rice, bread, sugar, cereal, candy bars and soft drinks, that the average American diet contains more than enough PCP to create the necessary buildup to cause cancer in ten years—unless we get it out of the food soon. Write your congressman!

What's Safe to Eat

Until we clean up our environment, we are faced with unnecessary risk. But a wise person learns to eat as many different foods as possible to allow the liver to detoxify each pollutant before it is stored in our fatty tissue. Eat well to help keep your liver and immune system healthy. Eat as many unprocessed foods as you can. Wash your raw foods well. Avoid the foods that flagrantly pollute—especially dyed foods. Learn to read labels. Help your body work properly by maintaining a good activity (exercise) level.

And above all—take vitamins. The next several chapters will discuss how vitamins can prevent or control cancer.

References

1. Houston, Donald. United States Department of Agriculture (USDA) press release, 13 October 1975.

2. Kelly, R. F. *Food Product Development*, September 1974.

1983 UPDATE

In 1978, Dr. P. Newberne directly implicated nitrites as carcinogens. The FDA examined his data and disagreed. However, free nitrites can produce nitrosamines, thus should be phased out of foods.

Part Two
NATURE'S OWN FIGHTERS— THE EVIDENCE

CHAPTER 8

Vitamin A

I am discussing vitamin A first, not because it is first in alphabetical order but because it is first in importance in protection against cancer. The value of vitamin A in preventing and perhaps curing cancer is finally being realized after decades of supporting research. In 1977 alone, Dr. Michael Sporn of the National Cancer Institute announced that the National Bladder Cancer Project plans to start clinical trials of a vitamin A derivative to see if it could lower the cancer incidence in several groups of cancer-prone individuals;[1] and Dr. Harold Manner of Loyola University in Chicago reported that vitamin A was a critical component of his protocol to *cure* breast cancer in mice.[2]

It was no accident that they were using vitamin A or vitamin A derivatives in their research. Researchers first noticed in 1925 that there was a relationship between a deficiency in vitamin A and cancer.

Several experiments from the 1930s through the 1950s confirmed this relationship and since then, researchers have learned that cancer-causing chemicals can react more strongly with DNA in vitamin A deficient cells, that cancers are hard to transplant into animals adequately nourished with vitamin A, and that vitamin A was therapeutic in precancerous cells.

Scientific optimism about the effectiveness of vitamin A started increasing in 1974. Science reporter Bernie Ward interviewed several researchers at the 1974 NCI conference for the *National Enquirer*. His questions led to some practical summations of the information exchanged. He quoted Dr. Frank Chytill of Vanderbilt University as saying, "Recent dramatic findings about vitamin A and its effects on cancer have opened up a whole new approach to cancer therapy. With vitamin A therapy, doctors now have a way to restore body cells to normal—rather than destroy them with surgery, chemotherapy or radiation. We now have laboratory evidence that cancers such as breast, lung, and skin tumors can be cured by treatment with vitamin A. . . . People can certainly cut their chances of getting cancer by making sure they are not deficient in vitamin A."

Dr. David Ong, a co-researcher of Dr. Chytill's at Vanderbilt, told reporter Ward: "We know that lack of vitamin A retards normal growth, weakens the mucous linings of the body and causes night blindness. But when the proper level of vitamin A is restored, the body returns to normal. Work with patients in Europe strongly indicates that vitamin A works the same way with cancer."

Dr. George Plotkin of the Massachusetts Institute of Technology added, "A deficiency of vitamin A prevents a mucous coating from forming on the trachea, lungs, rectum, digestive system and on the inside of the skin. The vitamin A deficiency doesn't cause cancer, but it makes these areas less able to resist cancer."

Dr. Plotkin and his colleague Dr. Paul Newberne reported that giving rats ten times their usual vitamin A intake dramatically slashed their susceptibility to lung cancer.

Dr. Michael Sporn of the National Cancer Institute sees the action of vitamin A as more than just the health of the mucous membranes.

In a December 1977, interview, Dr. Sporn discussed with me the effects of vitamin A deficiency and his tests of more efficient vitamin A derivatives. "If you are vitamin A deficient, there is no question that you may be more susceptible to development of cancer, but you do not need to take a lot of vitamin A to correct a deficiency. Any sort of multivitamin tablet will alleviate a deficiency state. That includes keeping your mucous membranes and respiratory tract in proper working order.

"I am not recommending that anybody take megadoses of vitamin A, but probably one of your best investments that you can make in your food budget is to spend a few cents a day and take a multivitamin capsule."

Dr. Sporn pointed out, "Well over half of all human cancer starts in epithelial tissue: the tissue that forms the lining of organs, forms glands such as mammary glands, skin, and passages in the body. The respiratory tract, the digestive tract, the urinary tract, and the reproductive tract are all lined with epithelial tissue. And *all* of the specialized cells that form epithelial tissue depend on vitamin A for their normal development.

"Dr. Umberto Saffioti and his collaborators showed that vitamin A had some ability to protect animals from development of lung cancer ten years ago, but they ran into a problem with toxicity trying to increase vitamin A's effectiveness. That is why it seemed logical to me to look for a synthetic derivative of vitamin A that would be a way around the toxicity problem.

"But as far as vitamin A deficiency is concerned, there is work way back in the 1920s by D. S. B. Wolbach of Harvard which suggests a relationship between vitamin A deficiency and cancer. Dr. Wolbach pointed out that there were similarities between the cancerous process and what goes on in tissues that are vitamin A deficient in terms of loss of control in cell differentiation. The problem that exists in cancer was pointed out over 50 years ago."

There is debate over how vitamin A and its derivatives control the early precancerous stages to prevent the development of cancer.

I asked Dr. Sporn if the retinoids (vitamin A and similar compounds) destroy a precancerous cell or just keep it from spreading.

Dr. Sporn's answer not only sheds light on how vitamin A works, but strengthens the contention that cancer can be prevented or slowed with vitamins.

"We don't have all the answers to that question so a lot of research is being done in that area now. None of the retinoids, if used appropriately, are cytotoxic (cell-killing) agents. You can kill a cell or a person with too much of anything—even salt or water. But one does not think of salt and water as toxic agents. Similarly, if used in sensible amounts, the retinoids are not toxic agents.

"They are hormone-like controllers of cell differentiation. The approach that we are trying to develop is to use them, not to kill cancer cells, but to control the differentiation of precancerous cells."

What Dr. Sporn means by cell differentiation: the cells stay in a mature differentiated state, rather than reverting to the undifferentiated cells that are characteristic of cancer.

Dr. Sporn further explained, "Now whether this actually arrests the process of development of cancer or whether this causes the precancerous cells to disappear from tissue is a topic of current research.

"If all that you do is just slow down this process of development of cancer so that instead of the typical twenty-year latent period from the time people may be first exposed to a carcinogen and the time that they develop cancer, you double that latent period, then there would be twenty additional years of good life that you would be offering people.

"Now in terms of modern surgery and chemotherapy, if they get an additional five years of survival, this is considered a very major achievement. So what we are really trying to do is to slow down or prevent the development of malignancy.

"If you slow it down enough, then for practical purposes it never occurs, although the basic process of development of cancer may still be going on, but at a very, very slow rate—such that it really never causes anyone any problems."

"The latent period is like a fire that is smoldering beneath the surface. It gives no symptoms; but if one goes and looks for precancerous (premalignant) cells, you can find evidence of the chronic disease process. The object of the preventive approach as I see it is to do something about the disease process when it is in this early smoldering stage, before you have the fire. Once you have invasive cancer, then you can't do prevention anymore. You have to change your approach.

"It's pretty clear that retinoids have a hormonelike action in controlling cell differentiation. Cancer would appear to be a disease in which the gene material, DNA, has been damaged by chemicals or radiation. Usually the damage will kill the cells, but sometimes the damage leads to cancer.

"Once DNA is damaged, cancer doesn't occur immediately. It can be twenty years after DNA damage occurs before malignancy develops."

Dr. Sporn takes great care to distinguish between natural vitamin A and the derivative that is being tested at the National Cancer Institute and other research centers.

"The word retinoid is just a generic word which describes a family of substances. Within this family there are hundreds of different individual compounds. Some of the individual compounds are the naturally occurring forms of vitamin A such as those we eat in our diet or take in vitamin pills.

"These natural forms of vitamin A are largely stored in the liver and if taken in excess, they can cause very severe liver damage and also cause other undesirable toxic side effects. There have been cases of people who have symptoms resembling brain tumor due to excessive dosages of vitamin A. Some people believe that if some is good, them some more is better. With massive amounts of vitamin A, they can get themselves into rather severe side effects."

"Also," Dr. Sporn points out, "vitamin A does not get into all the body parts in high enough concentrations that we want for effectiveness. If you were worried about the development of bladder cancer and took a large amount of vitamin A, this would be mostly stored in the liver and would not be getting additional vitamin A to your bladder.

"The synthetic retinoids work by the same mechanism as vitamin A, we believe, but there are two major differences: you can put the retinoids where they are needed in high concentration, and you can put them there safely."

Dr. Sporn has concentrated on the vitamin A derivative, the synthetic retinoid, 13-cis retinoic acid that he selected because of its effectiveness and lack of toxicity. The effectiveness has been shown in animal experiments and the safety has been documented in both animal and human tests. Still there is no solid evidence that 13-cis retinoic acid is capable of preventing cancer in man. That's why clinical trials with the National Bladder Cancer Project will be undertaken. It will probably be 1981 or so before we have significant data.

They will pick a group of people known to have an extremely high risk of developing a given type of cancer and provide them with daily supplements of 13-cis retinoic acid. The group will then be monitored for cancer incidence for two to five years and compared to a comparable group not receiving the supplements.

Examples of high risk groups are those with precancerous growths, a strong history of familial cancers, post-surgery lung cancer patients, heavy smokers and workers exposed to carcinogens such as asbestos and uranium. The first clinical trials will be to prevent bladder cancer.

The study will take place at five medical centers around the country: The Massachusetts General Hospital in Boston, the Medical College of Virginia in Richmond, the University of Iowa, Rush Presbyterian-St. Luke's in Chicago, and the Mason Clinic in Seattle.

Others are interested in the retinoids too. At a conference held on the prevention of cancer at the National Cancer Institute in Bethesda, Maryland in February 1978, several scientists explained their research. Dr. Richard C. Moon of the Illinois Institute of Technology has found that animals treated with carcinogens that normally cause lung or skin cancer are protected by retinoids. Dr. Warren Kountz of the Medical College of Virginia reported he was testing retinoids on bladder cancers, and Dr. Gordan Zubrod of the University of Miami School of Medicine reported he was testing retinoids on heavy smokers with precancerous cells in their respiratory tracts.

As Dr. Ong mentioned earlier, there have been reports of success in Europe with vitamin A against cancer.

Research by Drs. Hans Nieper, Karl Ransberger and H. Hoefer-Janker shows that an emulsified form of vitamin A can be given in large doses for brief periods with significant effect against cancer. The emulsified vitamin A is believed to be taken directly into the body's lymph system, thus bypassing the liver and rapidly building up blood levels to obtain the greatest therapeutic effect with tolerable toxicity. However, the toxicity, especially the long-term toxicity, has not been fully investigated as yet.

In the emulsified vitamin A (A-Mulsin) treatment, 30 million I.U. are given in gradually increasing doses over two to three weeks. However, toxicity symptoms are produced.

There are other lines of research that suggest that vitamin A may have more of a role than covered purely by mucous membrane health or cell differentiation.

A deficiency of vitamin A was shown to make animals more susceptible to carcinogens as early as 1944 by Nobel Prizewinner, E. V. Euler of Sweden.

Vitamin A was shown to strengthen cancer drugs such as Urethan as early as 1948.

The study of the relationship of vitamin A in protecting against experimentally induced cancer was published in 1959. The researchers studied oral cancer in hamsters given carcinogens known to produce oral cancers. Five groups of hamsters were given different levels of vitamin A supplementation, while all five groups were given the same level of carcinogen. The cancer incidence was greater in the groups with the lowest supplement. Thus the investigators concluded: "These data suggest that vitamin A deficiency increased the susceptibility of hamsters to carcinogen-induced benign and malignant tumors."[3]

Besides carcinogen-induced oral cancer prevention, in 1963, vitamin A was shown to cure and prevent leukoplakia (whitish warty patches in the mouth which may become cancerous).

In 1965, vitamin A was shown to greatly reduce the

number of cancers in various epithelial tissues of hamsters caused by a carcinogen and to reduce the number of cancers in the trachea and bronchi caused by a different carcinogen. Also, in 1967, vitamin A reduced skin cancer incidence in mice given a carcinogen.

In one of Dr. Umberto Saffioti's experiments when he was at the Chicago Medical School (he later joined the National Cancer Institute), 113 hamsters were dosed with the cigarette smoke carcinogen, benzopyrene. In the 53 control animals not given extra vitamin A protection, 16 developed lung cancer. However, in the 60 vitamin-A-treated animals, only one developed lung cancer and four developed benign tumors. Dr. Saffiotti had similar results with carcinogens that cause cancer in the stomach, gastro-intestinal tract and the uterine cervix.[4]

Vitamin A was found to have a therapeutic effect on premalignant lesions in 1970.[5]

Thus vitamin A has been shown in animal studies to be protective against some carcinogens whether a recognized deficiency exists or not, and to be therapeutic in the treatment of precancerous cells. It has not yet been demonstrated to be effective in any fully developed invasive cancer.

Dr. Raymond Shamberger of the Cleveland Clinic has done a series of animal tests which led him to conclude: "Vitamin A retards the growth and inhibits the induction of benign and malignant tumors."[6]

In several series of tests, Dr. Shamberger painted carcinogens on the skins of mice. When vitamin A was added to the carcinogen, the tumor incidence was reduced by up to 76 percent.

In 1971, Dr. K. K. Georgieff of Ste-Anne-de-Belleuve in Quebec reported that many synthetic and natural anticancer compounds were free-radical inhibitors. Vitamin A is a relatively strong free-radical inhibitor because of five double bonds.[7]

In 1972, Drs. Martin H. Cohen and Paul Carbone found that the potentiating antitumor effect of vitamin A (up to 100-fold) that had been reported when the vitamin was used with several antitumor drugs extended to the modern drug BCNU and in the treatment of leukemia as well.[8]

Dr. Martin Zisblatt and colleagues at the Albert Einstein College of Medicine in New York found that vitamin A was protective even in mice that develop tumors when injected with viral tumor extract. Typically, 40-50 percent tumor reduction was obtained with vitamin A supplementation.[9]

When cancers were transplanted to other mice, vitamin A inhibited the body's "taking" of the cancer transplant.

The survival time for mice inoculated with a million breast tumor cells increased by 50 to 70 percent with vitamin A. In animals inoculated with ten thousand cells, 50 percent normally develop cancer, but only 10 percent of the mice on vitamin A therapy developed tumors.

In 1974, Drs. Donald Hill and Tzu-Wen Shih postulated that vitamin A acts as a specific antioxidant and inhibits the intermediate compound ordinarily formed in the body from the carcinogen. Thus the carcinogen is inactivated.[10]

Scientific interest really perked up with these results, and a conference sponsored by the National Cancer Institute and Hoffmann-LaRoche, Inc. was held in Bethesda, Maryland, in November 1974.

The interest in the conference was sufficient to warrant a full report in *Science* by T. H. Maugh.[11] At the conference, David Kaufman of NCI discussed experiments that showed that carcinogens bind much more tightly to DNA from vitamin A-deficient animals, thus possibly increasing the odds of the vitamin A-deficient animal developing cancer. Dr. Kaufman has also demonstrated that when vitamin A is administered simultaneously, carcinogens are inhibited from binding to DNA.

Colon cancer was observed to be greater in vitamin A-deficient rats exposed to a carcinogen by Drs. Paul Newberne and Adrianne Rogers of the Massachusetts Institute of Technology. They also reported that giving rats ten times their usual vitamin A intake dramatically slashed their susceptibility to lung cancer.

Vitamin A was reported to reverse the effects of carcinogens in tissue cultures from the prostates of mice by Dr. Dharam Chopra of the Southern Research Institute in Birmingham.

His Southern Research Institute colleague, Dr. Donald Hill, informed the conference that vitamin A prevents the carcinogen benzopyrene from being converted in the liver to its damaging form, an epoxide.

The incidence of lung tumors was reduced by supplementation with vitamin A in rats fed a carcinogen, according to Dr. Paul Nettesheim of the Oak Ridge National Laboratory.

Even more encouragingly, Dr. Curtis Port of the Illinois Institute of Technology reported that vitamin A given after exposure to carcinogens inhibited the formation of lung cancer.

Confirmation that the transplant of cancer from one animal to another is virtually impossible if the second animal has adequate vitamin A levels was made by Hoffmann-La Roche's Dr. Richard Swarm.

In the following year, Dr. E. Bjelke of the Cancer Registry of Norway published his five-year study involving 8,278 male smokers. Dr. Bjelke found that 74 percent of the men with lung cancer were in the lowest third ranking according to vitamin A intake. He also found that vitamin A especially helped smokers living in cities. Vitamin A-deficient city dwellers have three times the lung cancer rate of better-nourished city dwellers.[12]

In 1976, Dr. Alex Sakula of Redhill General Hospital, Surrey, England, observed that blood levels of vitamin A were lower than normal in all of his twenty-eight bronchial cancer patients.[13]

Also in 1976, Dr. Bernard P. Lane of New York State University at Stonybrook exposed tissues from 200 trachea to a carcinogen for three weeks. The precancerous changes caused by the carcinogen were reversed with vitamin A treatment.[14]

The evidence showing that vitamin A and its derivatives have a role in helping us ward off cancer begins to be impressive. Vitamin A protects cells against invasion by keeping mucous membranes healthy, interferes with chemical attack on DNA and controls cell differentiation.

Here is a rare instance in nutrition where there is little argument. Many scientists are already convinced, thanks to decades of research on laboratory animals and epidemiological surveys.

A great number of Americans are deficient in vitamin A and at needless risk of cancer. While awaiting the final verdict of large-scale human testing, it may be very wise to maintain adequate levels of vitamin A.

References

1. Sporn, Michael. American Cancer Society Science Writers' Seminar. Sarasota, Florida, 4 April 1977.

2. Manner, Harold. National Health Federation Seminar. Chicago, September 1977.

3. Rowe and Corlin. *J. Dental Research*, 38: 72-83, 1959.

4. Saffioti, Umberto. *Cancer*, 20: 857-864, 1967.

5. Bollag, W. *Int. J. Vitamin Research*, 40: 299-313.

6. Shamberger, Raymond. *J. Nat. Cancer Inst.*, September 1971.

7. Georgieff, K. K. *Science,* 173:3996, 537-539, 6 August 1971.

8. Cohen, Martin H. and Carbone, Paul. *J. Nat. Cancer Inst.,* 48: 921-926, 1972.

9. Zisblatt, Martin et al. Reported in an article by M. Bricklin, *Prevention,* November 1975.

10. Hill, Donald and Tzu-Wen Shih. *Cancer Research,* 34: 564-570, March 1974.

11. Maugh, T. H. *Science,* 186: 4170, 1198, 1974.

12. Bjelke, E. *Int. J. Cancer,* 15, 1975.

13. Sakula, Alex. *British Med. J.,* 31 July 1976.

14. Lane, Bernard P. *Proceed. Amer. Assoc. Cancer Research,* March 1976.

1983 UPDATE

The March 19, 1981 issue of *Nature* published a review article that concluded, "Human cancer risks are inversely correlated with (a) blood vitamin A level and (b) dietary beta-carotene" (R. Peto et al.).

The November 28, 1981 issue of *Lancet* reported that the intake of beta-carotene was inversely related to the 19-year incidence of lung cancer in a prospective study of 1,954 middle-aged men (R. B. Shekelle et al.). Of the 33 subjects who developed lung cancer, 25 had diets low in beta-carotene.

When the participants were divided into four equal-sized groups based on their beta-carotene intake, the lung cancer incidence was 2.9 percent in the group with the lowest beta-carotene intake, 2.2 percent in the next lowest, 1.2 percent in the third group, and only 0.4 percent in the group with the highest beta-carotene intake.

A study published in the *Journal of Cancer* (R. Modan et al., 28:421–424, 1981) also confirmed that vitamin A has a protective effect.

Nutrition Reviews (40, (9):257–261, 1982) also considered the mounting reports.

CHAPTER 9

Vitamin C

WHILE vitamin A has been shown to be effective in preventing cancer and slowing the progress and spread of the cancerous process in animals, vitamin C (ascorbic acid or ascorbate) has been shown to help cure a percentage of "terminal" cancer patients in controlled clinical studies as well as have preventive action.

Vitamin C, like vitamin A, has several modes of action useful for preventing or controlling cancer. Vitamin C strengthens the body's defenses against cancer by increasing the effectiveness of the immune system that destroys cancer cells, and makes it more difficult for cancer cells to reproduce and spread by strengthening an intercellular material called "ground substance." Vitamin C also protects us against some cancer-causing chemicals such as nitrites (nitrosamines) and directly detoxifies still other carcinogens.

Although the U.S. taxpayers have spent over 800 million dollars directly on cancer research, another 200 million dollars on support programs, and several tens of millions in tax revenues through tax-deductible contributions to the American Cancer Society, the clinical trials of vitamin C were obtained without financial support. They were obtained as "bootleg" research. Today the research is being carried out still without a penny of U.S. funds, thanks to the Linus Pauling Institute and the Scottish Government.

What is this clinical evidence that has caused Dr. Linus Pauling, two-time Nobel Laureate, to conclude that "a high intake of vitamin C is beneficial to all patients with cancer"?

The hard evidence has been obtained thanks to a Scottish surgeon, Dr. Ewan Cameron, of Vale of Leven Hospital, Loch Lomondside, Scotland, and his colleagues. Drs. Cameron and Pauling jointly published a report on the beneficial effects of vitamin C on terminal cancer patients in 1976 in the *Proceedings of the National Academy of Science*.[1]

The Cameron and Pauling study compared 100 terminally ill patients given 10 grams (10,000 milligrams) per day to 1000 other such patients. Both groups were treated identically in all ways except one was not given the vitamin C. Both groups of patients were treated by the same physicians in the same hospital.

At the time the study report was prepared, those patients given vitamin C lived more than four times longer than the matched "control" patients. Since thirteen of the patients were still alive in January 1978, and twelve patients seemingly are free of cancer, the survival ratio is more than five times longer for the patients given vitamin C, and still improving. All of the 1000 "control" patients have died.

Sixteen of the 100 in the vitamin C group lived more than a year, as opposed to only three of the 1000 patients not given vitamin C.

These patients, now apparently healthy, were once considered terminal. The progress of their disease was such that in the considered opinion of at least two independent physicians, the continuance of any conventional form of treatment would offer no further benefit.

At the time of the 1976 report, thirteen vitamin C-treated colon cancer patients lived more than seven times as long as the 130 matched "control" patients. And their quality of life improved and pain lessened.

The 1976 report also indicated that the vitamin C-treated breast cancer patients lived six times longer than their matched "control" group, and vitamin C-treated kidney cancer patients lived five times longer.

Drs. Cameron and Pauling also noted that survival time was increased by a factor of at least 20 for some 10 percent of the patients. This caused them to wonder what the results would be if treatment were started earlier and if larger amounts of vitamin C were used.

At this writing over 500 patients with cancer, and some with cancer in its early stages, are being treated by Dr. Cameron and other physicians. Although the final results are not available yet, Dr. Pauling said there is nothing at the present time that suggests that the results won't be as good or better than those reported in 1976.

Yet as of early 1978, the National Cancer Institute has turned down Dr. Pauling's request for research grants for the fifth straight year.

In an April 1977 speech, Dr. Pauling commented,

In 1971, when Dr. Ewan Cameron began treating patients with advanced cancer by giving them sodium ascorbate, the improvement in health of the patients who received sodium ascorbate was so striking that in the spring of 1973 I went to the National Cancer Institute with case histories of the first 40 patients to have been treated this way, and asked the officials of the Institute to carry out a controlled trial. I was told that the National Cancer Institute would not carry out a controlled trial until animal studies had been made, and was invited to submit an application for support of such studies. I submitted the application, and three similar applications, during later years.

These grant applications were turned down. I now have another application pending—an application for support not only of animal studies, but also of basic scientific studies of the action of ascorbic acid, especially in relation to the immune process, and clinical studies in several hospitals. The developments in the field of ascorbic acid in relation to cancer during the past four years, especially the observations of Ewan Cameron and his associates, have been so striking as, in my opinion, to justify the allocation of a significant fraction of the total budget of the National Cancer Institute to the investigation of vitamin C and other vitamins in relation to the prevention and treatment of cancer.

I have received from Roger H. Halterman, Chief, Diagnosis and Treatment Branch, Division of Cancer Research Resources and Centers, NCI, a copy of the Summary Statement about the review by the Experimental Therapeutics Study Section of my grant proposal (reference 1 RO1 CA 21970-01). The first sentence of the Summary Statement is "Based on evaluation of scientific merit of this application, disapproval must be recommended."[2]

In a 1977 interview by the *Body Forum,* Dr. Pauling was asked how many lives could be saved with the use of vitamin C in cancer treatment.

Dr. Pauling replied, "In 1971 when I first suggested that vitamin C might be of use against cancer I estimated that it might save 10 percent of the people who die of cancer. The reason that I was saying that was, although there are some very good arguments why vitamin C might be effective, there was very little direct evidence. There was only some epidemiological evidence at that point. Now, 10 percent is 36,000 Americans a year, kept from dying of cancer. That's about a hundred a day. Today I'm around to saying that with proper use of vitamin C for cancer, we could cut the death rate by 75 percent. This would be 75 percent of 360,000 people who die every year of cancer. These are people's lives who could have been extended with the use of vitamin C."

The *Body Forum* interview then inquired if Dr. Pauling felt that vitamin C is the principal weapon against cancer.

"I don't think that anything will ever replace surgery when the cancer is operable. However, I don't believe that there have been any thorough studies on vitamin C as an alternative to high-energy radiation or the anti-cancer drugs. So, it will be necessary to make very careful studies of what the relationship of vitamin C and other nutritional therapy is to these conventional treatments.

"I think that it is probably wise for every cancer patient to receive vitamin C. There is always the possibility that other cancer treatments would interfere with the vitamin C, or the vitamin C would interfere with the cancer drug. These questions need to be examined. They haven't been up to this point. So, I would repeat that surgery is called for in a great many patients. The relationship of vitamin C to other ancillary treatments still needs further study.

"How much to take depends on whether you are in ordinary health with no signs of cancer or trying to fight cancer. Dr. Cameron gives his advanced cancer patients 10 grams a day. I don't know that that's the right dose. Perhaps it should be more. In my book, *Vitamin C and the Common Cold* (Freeman, 1970), I wrote that many persons could get by on 250 milligrams a day and I recommended a dose of 1 gram. I, myself, take 10 grams a day. I think that even though the National Cancer Institute has still not recognized the value of vitamin C, information about it appears to be spreading. I was told that when the new director of NCI, Dr. Arthur Upton, was interviewed and asked if he took vitamin C, he said yes, that he took 500 milligrams a day just on general principle, and partially because I recommended it. The former Assistant Secretary for Health, Dr. T. Cooper, was reported in the *Medical Tribune* as saying that he took 1,500 milligrams of vitamin C a day and that he gave his family large doses of vitamin C. He believed that larger intakes of vitamin C were valuable not only against colds, but possibly also against cancer. He is now the dean of the Medical School at Cornell University. So, there are plenty of important medical people who are beginning to accept the idea."

Irwin Stone, who is credited with getting Dr. Pauling interested in vitamin C research, has commented about dosages of vitamin C for cancer patients.[3]

Mr. Stone first comments on a case history from one of Dr. Cameron's reports, involving a "treatable" cancer in a 42-year-old long-haul truck driver. The diagnosis was malignant lymphoma, and arrangements were started to have him treated by orthodox irradiation and cytoxic chemotherapy.

"Because of an administrative delay in sending him to the appropriate facility and his rapid clinical deterioration, ascorbate was administered in the hope the malignant growth could be slowed until conventional treatment could be started. He was given 10,000 milligrams a day intravenously for the first ten days, and 10,000 milligrams a day orally thereafter. The response to the IV ascorbate was so dramatic that the patient 'claimed to feel quite fit and well and had been transformed from a dying into a recovering situation. Appetite had returned, night sweats had ceased, with a general sense of well-being.' The enlarged liver and spleen had receded, and other symptoms of the disease rapidly subsided. The 10,000 milligrams of oral ascorbate were continued for five months, and during this time he remained well and in active employment. At this time, for some unknown reason, the oral ascorbate was stopped. A month later at a routine clinical examination, he was sick and complained of a recurrence of the symptoms. Clinical evidence of return of the disease was obtained. Ascorbic acid at 10,000 milligrams a day orally was again given, but without the previous dramatic response. Two weeks later the disease had so progressed that he was readmitted to the hospital and given 20,000 milligrams a day of ascorbate intravenously for two weeks, and 12,500 milligrams a day orally thereafter. A slow, sustained clinical improvement was shown, and examination about six months later showed him normal in all respects. 'The patient remains fit and well, is in active heavy employment, continues to take 12,500 milligrams of vitamin C a day, and has no evidence of active disease.' "

This case was described in detail because of the similarities of response to stopping the daily intake of ascorbate as in a case of myelogenous leukemia. In both patients, the cancerous disease went into remission during the large daily intakes of vitamin C, and the disease returned as soon as the daily intake ceased. Control of the disease occurred when vitamin C was started again. In the truck driver's case, the response was not so dramatic on reinstating the ascorbate as in the leukemia case. It is likely this was because the truck driver was getting much less ascorbate than the leukemic—12,500 milligrams for the truck driver as compared with 24,500 to 42,000 milligrams a day in the leukemic.

Mr. Stone adds, "A dose of 12,500 milligrams of vitamin C is in the lower fringes of the therapeutic effectiveness for a disease as serious and stressful as cancer. Daily intakes of vitamin C of at least 50,000 milligrams a day will give a more effective therapeutic response, as indicated not only by this leukemic case, but also by unpublished clinical data of Dr. William Saccoman of San Diego, discussed later. Doses of this order of magnitude can be given without fear of toxic responses. Dr. Fred Klenner of Reidsville, North Carolina, uses up to 300,000 milligrams of sodium ascorbate intravenously each day in his successful therapy of viral diseases.

"Drs. Cameron and Baird, in 1973, published the important observation that intravenous megadoses of sodium ascorbate will relieve pain in terminal cancer patients. Five patients on a heavy morphine schedule to control pain were able to discontinue the morphine entirely within a few days after the 10,000 milligrams of sodium ascorbate injections were started. A similar pain-killing effect was noted many years ago by Klenner in his megascorbic therapy of severe burns and snakebite. No withdrawal symptoms occurred in Cameron and Baird's patients when the morphine was stopped. This would suggest that megadoses of sodium ascorbate might be useful in the control of drug-abuse, and the salvage of addicts.

"In addition to the aforementioned published data on ascorbate and cancer, some unpublished work is being conducted which will be briefly mentioned. Dr. Virginia Livingston and her group in San Diego are using 10 to 50 grams a day of ascorbate in conjunction with other cancer modalities with very exciting clinical responses. Dr. Saccoman has been interested in megascorbic therapy for many years, and in fact independently observed some years ago, the pain-killing and morphine-substituting effects of intravenous sodium ascorbate in terminal cancer, reported in 1973.

"From his wide clinical experience, Dr. William J. Saccoman has evolved this general procedure: patients are started with 22,500 milligrams of intravenous sodium ascorbate daily. They also take oral ascorbic acid and sodium ascorbate to a total of 50 grams (50,-000 mg) ascorbate a day, or until diarrhea results. The diarrhea clears in a few days, if present, and oral intake is increased gradually along with a decrease in intravenous administration. The total daily dosage is kept at 50 grams a day of ascorbate until the patient is entirely upon oral administration. The first noticeable effect is an almost immediate improvement in the patient's well-being. The following are a couple of case histories, typical of the clinical data being obtained:

"1. An adult male had bladder cancer which metastasized to the spine at the level of the tenth thoracic vertebra.

"Surgical removal of this spinal cancer left the patient completely paraplegic. He was put on 50,-000 mg of ascorbate, and to quote the doctor, 'he is now coming along beautifully.'

"There has been a return of bladder and bowel function and the patient is able to walk with braces. The cancers are under control, and dormant. During the day, the patient takes the powdered ascorbic acid and sodium ascorbate, and at bedtime takes eight timed-release ascorbic acid tablets.

"2. An adult woman was diagnosed as having carcinoma of the lung which had metastasized to the thoracic duct. This caused so much fluid to collect in the chest cavity as to interfere with breathing, requiring 11 fluid drainages of the chest cavity. This cancerous invasion also caused giant ascites in the abdomen, so big as to cause an umbilical hernia requiring surgical repair. Three years ago she was put on ascorbate, about 50,000 mg a day, and has been taking it ever since. The fluid in the lung and the ascites cleared and there are no longer any signs of these. Although the lung tumor is still present and visible in X rays, it is starting to calcify, and there are no signs of active disease."

"The simple lesson of the work of Dr. Saccoman and the other investigators using these huge daily intakes of vitamin C is that the stresses of cancer increase the body's need for vitamin C to such an extent that these huge daily amounts are required merely to satisfy these vital needs. The body has great recuperative powers, and if these daily needs are not adequately filled, handicapping of the body's natural ability to resist and fight off the disease and heal itself results. Surgery, radiation, and chemotherapy only further increase the needs and requirements for more vitamin C. The first step in any therapy should be to give and supply enough daily vitamin C to aid the body to combat and overcome these stresses."

Keep in mind that possible needs for fighting diseases are vastly different than normal everyday needs for optimum health.

Earlier Studies

Why did Dr. Cameron try vitamin C? What indications did Dr. Pauling have that vitamin C would help cancer survival?

In 1951, it was established that cancer patients had lower than average amounts of vitamin C in their blood plasma and white blood corpuscles. Thus, they can't destroy cancer cells.

In 1948, epidemiologists Drs. Chope and Breslow interviewed 577 older residents of San Mateo County, California. When they followed up the interviews eight years later they found the death rate for those with the highest amounts of dietary vitamin C was less than half (40 percent) of those getting lesser amounts of vitamin C. This was true for the cancer death rate as well.[4]

Irwin Stone reported that German physicians, Drs. W. G. Deucher (1940), Von Wendt (1949), and L. Huber (1953) used 1 and 2 gram doses of vitamin C (with and without vitamin A) with good results.[5]

Mr. Stone also reported that in 1954 Dr. W. J. McCormick found that "the degree of malignancy is determined inversely by the degree of connective tissue resistance which in turn is dependent upon the adequacy of vitamin C status."

Earlier, in 1948, Drs. Goth and Littmann found that "cancers most frequently originate in organs whose vitamin C levels are below 4.5 mg percent and rarely grow in organs containing vitamin C above this concentration."[6]

In 1966, Dr. Cameron had published his book (*Hyaluronidase and Cancer,* Pergamon, 1966) outlining his views that strengthening the intercellular ground substance (the material that holds tissue cells together and is often called cellular cement) would prevent infiltration of cancer cells. He had noticed that cancer cells produced an enzyme, hyaluronidase, that attacked this intercellular cement and allowed the cancer to invade surrounding tissues.

In 1971, Dr. Cameron read of Dr. Pauling's comments that vitamin C increased the rate of collagen production, which strengthened the intercellular cement. This stimulated Dr. Cameron to begin cautiously treating cancer patients with vitamin C, and the two researchers joined on some projects. One of Dr. Cameron's first observations was that vitamin C reduced the patients' pain and improved their sense of well-being, appetite and mental alertness. Patients who had been receiving large doses of morphine or diamorphine no longer needed the pain-killing drugs.

In 1973, Norwegian researcher Dr. Bjelke surveyed 30,000 people and found that the greater the intake of vitamin C, the smaller the incidence of cancer—as Drs. Chope and Breslow had found in 1948.[7]

In 1969, Dr. Dean Burk of the National Cancer Institute found that vitamin C caused changes in cultures of cancer cells that destroyed them, while being harmless to normal cells. Dr. Burk concluded, "the future of effective cancer chemotherapy will not rest on the use of host-toxic compounds now so widely employed, but upon virtually host-nontoxic compounds that are lethal to cancer cells, of which vitamin C represents an excellent prototype example."[8]

Later that year, Dr. J. U. Schlegel of the Tulane University School of Medicine showed that bladder cancer due to smoking could be prevented by vitamin C.[9] His more recent report will be discussed later.

Perhaps somewhat related is the work relating vitamin C to the cure of rectal polyps. After taking 3 grams of vitamin C daily, rectal polyps disappeared in five of eight patients, while improving the condition of the other three.[10] In 1977, a West Virginia University researcher reported similar success. Of six patients, polyps disappeared in two patients, were reduced in three others and were not affected in the sixth.[11] Irwin Stone suggests that higher vitamin C intake or the use of a 3 percent sodium ascorbate enema in addition to the oral intake would have improved the results.

Increased Immunity

In response to questions about the Cameron and Pauling report, Dr. Paul Chretien, Chief of Tumor Immunology in the Surgical Branch of the National Cancer Institute, replied, "It is possible they did arrest the progress of tumor growth with massive doses of vitamin C. National Cancer Institute research has shown that vitamin C given to healthy patients stimulates the body's defense system and this usually means an increased immune response."

Dr. Chretien was referring to research he has conducted along with his NCI colleague, Dr. T. F.

Tehniger, and Dr. Robert Yonemoto, Director of Surgical Laboratories at the City of Hope National Medical Center in Duarte, California. The researchers were trying to overcome a perplexing problem of cancer surgery. Immediately after the surgical removal of malignant tumors, the immune system is very weak. Often cancer cells spill into the bloodstream during surgery, and when the immune response is weak the spilled cancer cells spread secondary cancers (metastases) throughout the body.

The group published a study in 1976 that showed 5 grams of vitamin C daily increased the production of lymphocytes (white blood corpuscles without granules) when the body was threatened by a foreign substance, and that 10 grams daily produced an even greater effect.[12] Cancer patients have a poor ability to make new lymphocytes, and their ability to survive is in line with their ability to produce lymphocytes.

The study was with healthy volunteers, and the researchers are now studying cancer patients to see if the same results can be observed.

Note that all studies discussed so far have been with people. Normally, preliminary cancer research is carried out with laboratory animals such as rats and mice, but there is a great difference, with respect to vitamin C, between humans and most animals. Most animals make their own vitamin C, or at least make most of what they need. Man, primates, guinea pigs, and a few other animals cannot produce vitamin C because of the lack of the required enzyme, believed to be caused by a genetic abnormality developed during evolution.

The guinea pig is a suitable experimental animal for vitamin C research, but not much is known about cancer in guinea pigs.

Dr. George Feigen, professor of Physiology at Stanford University, is studying the effects of vitamin C on the immune system of guinea pigs. Dr. Feigen has observed a large increase in the production of one of the components of the immune response.[13]

Previously researchers at the Bowman Gray School of Medicine in Winston-Salem, North Carolina, reported that vitamin C "turned on" the immune response. At the June 1971 meeting of the American Society of Biological Chemists held in San Francisco, Drs. Lawrence R. DeChatelet, Charles E. McCall and M. Robert Cooper reported that adding vitamin C to test tube mixtures of white blood corpuscles and bacteria stimulated increased activity of the white blood corpuscles. Without the added vitamin C, engulfment of the bacteria by the white blood corpuscles can take place, but they cannot break down the bacteria.

All of the preceding reports illustrate that vitamin C boosts immunity, which is the body's last line of defense against cancer.

The cell membrane is our first line of defense, and vitamin E is important to the health of the cell membrane. The next defensive barrier is the intercellular ground substance, the material that fills the interspace and isolates each cell from its neighbor. Vitamin C also stimulates interferon which offers a line of defense. Interferon is a protein that inhibits viral reproduction and is produced naturally by our cells when under viral attack.

Cell Protection

The environment of the cell influences its behavior. Tissue cells are imbedded in ground substance, a complex gel containing water, electrolytes, metabolites, dissolved gases, trace minerals, vitamins, enzymes, carbohydrates, fats and proteins. The gel is made viscous by long polymers and a three-dimensional network of collagen fibers.

It is important that the ground substance maintains

its very high viscosity and cohesiveness. This high viscosity physically restrains the cells from proliferating. When the cells need to proliferate, they release the enzyme hyaluronidase, which reduces the viscosity of the ground substance in the vicinity of the cell, allowing it to proliferate.

Dr. Cameron has proposed that cancer cells have the ability to continuously produce the enzyme hyaluronidase. As mentioned earlier, vitamin C helps keep the ground substance at the proper consistency. There is also evidence that vitamin C can inhibit or slow the production of hyaluronidase. Thus vitamin C helps keep the lid on cancer cells.[14]

Detoxification

Besides stimulating the immune response and strengthening the ground substance, vitamin C helps protect us from cancer by destroying chemicals known to cause cancer. The common meat preservative, nitrite, is converted to one of the group of carcinogens called nitrosamines in the stomach. Vitamin C blocks this reaction according to Dr. Sidney Mirvish and his colleagues at the University of Nebraska Medical Center.[15] The amounts of nitrites used for meat preservation is in excess of what is required and should be lessened. Perhaps vitamin C should be added to the meats to insure that vitamin C is available in the stomach when nitrite-containing foods are eaten.

As early as 1943 it was known that vitamin C could destroy common carcinogens such as benzopyrene which is found in cigarette smoke.[16]

Dr. J. U. Schlegel of Tulane University School of Medicine reported at the Second International Conference on vitamin C held in New York City in October 1974, that vitamin C prevented recurrences of bladder cancer. Earlier Dr. Schlegel had found that vitamin C in the urine interferes with the conversion of 3-hydroxy-anthranilic acid to cinnabaric acid and also interferes with the activity of any cinnabaric acid already present. The presence of vitamin C encourages the metabolic oxidation of 3-hydroxyanthranilic acid to amino-3 carboxymuconic acid. The high incidence of bladder cancer among heavy smokers can be explained by the fact that their blood and urine are often deficient in vitamin C and high in cinnabaric acid.[17]

In a June 1973 *American Laboratory* article, "Cancer, New Directions," I suggested to nutritionists that they consider the "after-protection" of nutrients. Nutrient antioxidants (vitamins C and E) should be taken often and in excess deliberately to ensure that some will be excreted. A moderate excess was defined as being well above present nutritional standards but well short of causing medical problems. If excesses are excreted, they will be available in the bladder and colon to protect against carcinogen formation. As just described, vitamin C, which is water-soluble, can protect the bladder, and vitamin E, which is fat-soluble and incompletely absorbed in the intestine, can protect the colon.

Vitamin C also protects the body from the harmful effects of acetaldehyde, a toxic substance in cigarette smoke. Acetaldehyde also accumulates in people who drink heavily. Acetaldehyde is more toxic than alcohol and has been implicated in the development of heart disease[18] and lung cancer.[19] Dr. Herbert Sprince and his colleagues at the Veterans Administration and Jefferson Medical College (Philadelphia, Pennsylvania) found that vitamin C protected rats against a considerable amount of otherwise toxic acetaldehyde.[20]

Dr. W. Robert Bruce, of the Ontario Cancer Institute and the University of Toronto, told a 1977 meeting of the American Chemical Society that he can reduce by 75 percent the number of potentially cancer-causing compound fragments found in the human bowel simply by adding vitamin C to the diet.

Vitamin C also reduces chromosome damage in tissue cultures.

Leukemia

Leukemia is a term that covers a group of diseases characterized by uncontrolled white blood corpuscle production. It is a form of cancer that does not involve uncontrolled tumor growth, but diseased white blood corpuscles and cells.

Leukemics have little vitamin C in their blood. Mr. Irwin Stone explains, "It is not only the biochemical stresses of the leukemic disease which lowers the plasma vitamin C levels, but also the abnormally large volumes of white blood cells which scavenge and remove the remaining vitamin C from the blood serum. The white blood cells, which selectively absorb up to forty times more vitamin C from the blood serum than the red blood cells, do a fine job of removing the final traces of vitamin C from the blood serum and trap it within their cells and make it unavailable to the tissues.

"The fact that there is no vitamin C left in the blood plasma deprives the tissues of the body of this most important and essential metabolite. The synthesis of collagen, in the tissues, for maintaining the strength of the tissues, blood vessels and capillaries is dependent on an adequate supply of vitamin C in the blood plasma. If the blood plasma is deficient in vitamin C, collagen production will stop and the mechanical strength of tissues, blood vessels and capillaries will weaken and hemorrhage will result.

"It is no wonder that what kills most leukemics is not the neoplastic disease itself, but hemorrhage and infection . . . If we can prevent them from dying of the manifestations of scurvy, it may be found that leukemia itself may not be such a serious fatal disease after all."[21]

Dr. Benjamin V. Siegel of the University of Oregon Medical School Department of Pathology, found that vitamin C markedly increased the interferon levels in leukemic mice.[22]

Skin Cancer

Vitamin C along with vitamin E reduces sun-caused damage to the skin that leads to skin cancer, according to dermatologists Drs. So Wan-Bang I o and Homer S. Black of the Baylor College of Medicine. They found that sunlight oxidized skin cholesterol to cholesterol alpha oxide, a known carcinogen. Vitamins C and E together with a synthetic antioxidant prevented the formation of cholesterol alpha-oxide. Whether or not this will protect against skin cancer or not has not been determined.[23]

Conclusions

Nobel Laureate Dr. Albert Szent-Györgyi puts vitamin C into proper perspective. "The medical profession itself took a very narrow and very wrong view. Lack of vitamin C caused scurvy, so if there was no scurvy there was no lack of vitamin C. Nothing could be clearer. The only trouble was that scurvy is not a first symptom of lack but a final collapse, a premortal syndrome, and there is a very wide gap between scurvy and full health."[24]

It has been shown that vitamin C increases immunity, reduces the ability of cancer cells to spread and detoxifies carcinogens.

Drs. Cameron and Pauling have shown the survival time of terminal cancer patients is increased four times and their quality of life is better with 10 grams of vitamin C daily.

There are many reasons why cancer patients should include vitamin C in their therapy. It is interesting to note that most of the cancer patients claiming that they have successfully controlled their cancer with Laetrile also include large amounts of vitamin C and other nutrients in their program. Is "natural remission" just other words for treatment with supernutrition?

References

1. Pauling, Linus and Cameron, Ewan. *Proceed. Nat. Acad. Science*, 73: 10, 3685-3689, October 1976.

2. Pauling, Linus. Par. 1: from comments prepared for the National Cancer Institute and given in several presentations including at the American Chemical Society meeting, April 1977. Par. 2: added at the National Nutritional Foods Association meeting in Las Vegas, July 1977.

3. Stone, Irwin. *American Laboratory*, September 1976.

4. Chope and Breslow. *Amer. J. Public Health*, 46: 61-67, 1955.

5. Stone, Irwin. *The Healing Factor: Vitamin C Against Disease*. New York: Grosset & Dunlap, 1972.

6. Goth, A. and Littmann, I. L. *Cancer Research*, 8: 349-351, 1948.

7. Bjelke, E. Reported by Linus Pauling. *Executive Health*, 13:4, p. 3, January 1977.

8. Burk, Dean. *Oncology*, 23: 33-43, 1969.

9. Schlegel, J. U. *J. Urology*, 101: 317-324, 1969.

10. *Surgery*, November 1975.

11. *Prevention*, p. 73, July 1977.

12. Yonemoto, R. H. Chretien, P. B. and Fehniger, T. F. *Amer. Soc. Clin. Oncology*, 288, 1976.

13. Feigen, George. *Executive Health*, 13 January, 1977.

14. Cameron, Ewan. *Oncology*, 27:2, 181-192, 1973.

15. Mirvish, Sidney *et al. Science*, 177: 65-68, 1972.

16. Warren, F. L. *Biochem. J.*, 37, 338-341, 1943.

17. Pelletier, O. *Amer. J. Clin. Nutr.*, 23:5, 520-524, 1970.

18. Passwater, Richard. *Supernutrition for Healthy Hearts.* New York: Jove, 1978.

19. ——*Supernutrition: The Megavitamin Revolution.* New York: Pocket Books, 1976.

20. Sprince, Herbert *et al. Executive Health,* January 1977.

21. Stone, Irwin. *Cancer Control Journal,* 2:1, 1-4, 1974.

22. Siegel, Benjamin V. *Infection and Immunity,* August 1974.

23. Wan Bang Lo, S. and Black, Homer S. *Nature,* 21 and 28 December 1973.

24. Szent-Györgyi, Albert. Personal letter, 19 March 1973.

1983 UPDATE

For more details on the role of vitamin C in combating cancer, please read *Cancer and Vitamin C* by Drs. Ewan Cameron and Linus Pauling (Warner Books, New York 1981).

The life-extending benefit of vitamin C in cancer patients reported by Drs. Cameron and Pauling has been confirmed in a Japanese study by Drs. Akira Murata and Fukumi Morishige of Saga University presented at the International Conference on Nutrition held in Tianjin, China, in June 1981. Those cancer patients who received 5 to 30 grams of vitamin C daily as their only therapy lived an average of 6.2 times as long as those on a dosage of 4 grams or less per day. Those suffering from cancer of the uterus lived an average of 15.4 times longer than those who had received little or no vitamin C (*Medical Tribune,* July 22, 1981).

A trial at the Mayo Clinic found no benefit from vitamin C (E.T. Creagan et al., *New Eng. J. Med.* 301:687–690, 1979). Dr. Pauling discounts this study due to the fact that the patients had had chemotherapy and hence were burnt-out immunologically.

Low vitamin C has been associated with cervical cancer (*Amer. J. Epidem.* 114:714, 1981) and breast cancer (*Med. World News* 56, 5/11/81).

CHAPTER 10

Vitamin E

VITAMIN E has been shown to help prevent cancers caused by many chemicals in our environment. This is important because, as discussed in earlier chapters, scientists estimate that 80 to 95 percent of human cancers are caused by the chemical carcinogens in the environment.

In addition to its protective role against cancer, vitamin E has been shown to lessen the harmful effects of the widely used anticancer drug Adriamycin. Previously, the drug had limited usage because of its harmful side effects. Now in combination with vitamin E, more effective dosages can safely be given to more people.

Also, additional vitamin E is required by those who overconsume polyunsaturated oils on many low-cholesterol diets. These oils have been shown to be cofactors in potentiating the effect of other cancer-causing chemicals.

Vitamin E gives us a second chance by stimulating our immune response, which can destroy precancerous cells before they turn into a malignancy.

From 1969 through 1972, I had experimented with

several combinations of the natural antioxidant nutrients plus some synthetic antioxidants. Vitamins A, C and E, and the mineral selenium are called antioxidants because they protect body cells against unwanted reactions with oxygen, but allow the desirable oxygen reactions to proceed without interference. I have been issued patents in several countries on these synergistic antioxidant formulations.

In the June 1973 issue of *American Laboratory,* I discussed my research in combining dietary antioxidants synergistically to reduce chemically induced cancers in mice to only 5 to 15 percent of the expected level. This research blossomed out of experiments in retarding the aging process.

During my longevity experiments, I noticed that the mice on high levels of antioxidant nutrients not only lived longer and in better overall health, but they were essentially free of tumors. This raised the question as to whether the increased longevity was due to retarding the aging process or to reducing cancer in a strain of mice particularly susceptible to cancer, or both. Subsequent experiments showed that the antioxidants slowed the aging process as a secondary factor and prevented cancer as a primary factor.

Test Results

Dr. Ray Shamberger, of the Cleveland Clinic Foundation, has completed several experiments with either vitamin E or selenium (which are interchangeable in some body functions but not all). These studies showed significant reduction of dimethylbenz(a)anthracene (DMBA)-induced cancers in mice. Cancer reduction was accomplished by either dietary supplementation of selenium or by application of either selenium or vitamin E to the skin area painted with DMBA several days previously. Cancer reduction varied with vitamin E or selenium concentration.

In one experiment to determine the extent of cancer-causing damage done by DMBA, Dr. Shamberger found that vitamin E reduced this damage by 63.2 percent and vitamin C by 31.7 percent.[1]

Dr. S. Jaffe has reported reduction of methylcholanthracene (MCA)-induced cancer by wheat germ oil (rich in vitamin E). Vitamin E proved effective in reducing cancers from injected MCA.[2] However, Dr. S. S. Epstein found that vitamin E and several other antioxidants were not effective in reducing dibenzpyrene (BP)-induced cancers.[3] More recently, Dr. Lee W. Wattenberg of the University of Minnesota Medical School had great success with synthetic antioxidants in reducing BP- or DMBA-induced stomach cancers. BP-induced cancers were reduced from 100 percent incidence in controls to 17 percent with 5mg/g of one antioxidant and to 22 percent with 5 mg/g of another antioxidant.[4]

Drs. S. Wan-Bang Lo and H. Black of the Baylor College of Medicine have found that antioxidant therapy does protect against sun-induced cancer. They found that after human or animal skin was exposed to ultraviolet light, cholesterol in the skin was oxidized to a compound called cholesterol alpha-oxide. Drs. Lo and Black reasoned that the cholesterol alpha-oxide could be the carcinogen and wondered if the use of antioxidants could prevent the formation of cholesterol alpha-oxide. They found that vitamin C, vitamin E and synthetic antioxidants did prevent the formation of cholesterol alpha-oxide and, more significantly, seemed to prevent skin cancer without causing any side effects.[5]

At this point it is obvious that a well-balanced diet, supplying all of the vitamins and trace minerals required, will be helpful in preventing some types of cancers. A reasonable person might conclude that it would make sense to take extra amounts of vitamin E as well. But there is still more evidence to consider, and yet other ways that vitamin E helps prevent cancer.

How Antioxidant Nutrients Work

Antioxidants such as vitamins A, C, and E and the mineral selenium protect the body against cancer in several ways. They protect the cell membrane against invasions by cancer-causing chemicals, protect DNA from being damaged, stimulate the immune response, and protect cells against radiation.

Membranes

The membranes are primary suspects for allowing normal cells to become abnormal. The membranes contain a large amount of lipids (phospholipids) and thus are subject to free-radical attack and peroxidation. Without adequate antioxidant protection (primarily from vitamin E), the membrane surface can be altered. Topographical "holes" or "gaps" in the distribution of electronic charges could result in abnormal cellular chemistry. I believe that the regulation of nutrients through the membrane is altered, encouraging either death (as in aging) if the nutrients cannot pass through the altered membrane, or irregular growth (as in cancer) if the nutrients enter into the cell uncontrollably. With the membrane surface altered, rapid growth may not be halted by feedback mechanisms dependent upon surface sensing. The ability of cells to recognize each other and maintain normal tissue patterns depends on the structural and immunological specificity of the cell surface. Also, membrane alterations may weaken antigens, thus causing the immune system to fail in its capacity to reject tumors.

Dr. Robert Franklyn of Los Angeles reported that a synthetic antioxidant seems to prevent cancer in cancer-prone dogs. Inbred Scottish deerhounds die of bone cancer between the ages of four to six years. In a controlled study, eighteen untreated deerhounds died on schedule between the ages of four to six. Another eighteen deerhounds got 30 grams a day of a synthetic antioxidant. They lived to age nine to ten and died of causes other than cancer.[6]

Protection of DNA

A third possible mechanism to explain the protective effect of antioxidant free-radical scavengers in preventing cancers is their binding to DNA, thus protecting DNA from alteration by carcinogens. Carcinogens have been shown to modify DNA by substitution on one of the constituent nucleotides. Aflatoxin B-1, a liver carcinogen, combines with DNA and reduces its primary activity with RNA polymerase.

Free-radical scavengers could react with the carcinogen to prevent the alteration of DNA, or the antioxidant itself could loosely bind with DNA or protein material. The loosely bound protector could not alter the DNA or protein.

Peroxidation

Free radicals are produced by several processes in the body. The healthy body normally can neutralize the self-produced free radicals before an excessive rate of damage occurs. However, polyunsaturated fatty acids form highly reactive self-propagating free radicals when initiated by a "starter" free radical. Whenever the intake of polyunsaturated fatty acids greatly exceeds that necessary for function, the risk of lipid peroxidation increases. Today's trend toward increasing the ratio of polyunsaturated fats to saturated fats needs close examination if this is true. In my book *Supernutrition for Healthy Hearts*, I have elaborated on this concern, along with my belief that normal diets may be unbalanced by the efforts to avoid dietary cholesterol.

Cholesterophobia, the needless fear of cholesterol by healthy people, has caused many people to increase their polyunsaturated fat intake far beyond that which the body can safely handle. The "average" American today ingests about two to three times the amount of polyunsaturated fat than Americans of sixty years ago—who were free of coronary thrombosis. A large number of studies alarmingly show proportionate increases in cancer (especially mammary) with increasing dietary polyunsaturate levels. Epidemiological studies of several countries show high cancer incidence in countries where considerable quantities of fish and few eggs and dairy products are consumed. Drs. M. L. Pearce and S. Dayton have reported that humans fed four times the polyunsaturates of controls developed a significantly higher number of cancers; 31 of 174 as opposed to 17 of 178.[7]

At least fourteen tests show a similar relationship.

At the 1977 meeting of the American Chemical Society in Chicago, Dr. S. P. Yang, Professor of Food and Nutrition at Texas Tech University, reported that rats fed a diet high in corn oil, which is relatively unsaturated, were more susceptible to cancer than rats fed a diet high in tallow, which is highly saturated.

Dr. Yang noted that his results confirmed various studies conducted over thirty years, that rats and mice fed certain vegetable oils were more prone to develop tumors than animals fed comparable diets containing animal fats.

In experiments conducted by Dr. Yang and his

coworkers, Drs. Harry Sproat, Cecil Felkner and Carmen Castro, groups of rats were fed diets for eight months containing, variously, 5 percent corn oil, 20 percent corn oil, 5 percent tallow, and 20 percent tallow. Rats were then challenged with the cancer-causing chemical AcAF. The rats on the 20 percent corn oil diet had the most cancers, with the 5 percent corn oil diet group next.[8]

Also in 1977, Boston University School of Medicine researchers, Drs. Sara Rothman and Selwyn Broitman, found that the carcinogen dimethylhydrozine, known as a cause of bowel cancer, created a higher incidence of cancer in rats fed diets high in polyunsaturated fats, compared to rats fed diets high in saturated fats.[9]

This is not to say polyunsaturates cause cancer. It is to emphasize the need for a balanced diet and the use of antioxidants with polyunsaturates. Nor is it to say that polyunsaturates are harmful or that they should necessarily be reduced if one's diet is balanced. It is important to have adequate polyunsaturates for proper nutrition—about 2 to 4 percent of the diet. Some people do not get enough of the essential polyunsaturate linoleic acid, or its precursor, arachidonic acid. But extreme measures to drastically change the polyunsaturate/saturate ratio, especially with unbalanced antioxidants, appear to create a great risk.

It should be stated here that a *continued* intake of vitamin E is required because the polyunsaturates stay in the body so long. The vitamin E can be used up while the polyunsaturates remain available.

Typical animal experiments show that DMBA-induced cancer rates increase with polyunsaturates and decrease with added vitamin E. Dr. Shamberger found that adding corn oil to the DMBA carcinogen promoter, croton resin, greatly increased the number of cancers. Applying either selenium, vitamin E or vitamin C several days later reduced the number of cancers. Saturated oils did not increase the cancer incidence.[10] Dr. Denham Harman has recently presented data showing that vitamin E decreased the tumor incidence among rats on a diet containing safflower oil as the sole source of lipid.[11]

A postulated mechanism involves peroxide-induced binding of a carcinogen to DNA. Another mechanism involving lipid peroxidation would be the attack of membranes by the lipid peroxides. The antioxidants would prevent both the initiation of lipid peroxidation and the propagation of peroxide radicals. The role of vitamin E as a free-radical scavenger in biological systems which initiate radical-mediated reactions has been researched extensively by Dr. P. McCoy of the Oklahoma Medical Research Foundation. He has found vitamin E to be very effective.

Radiation

Animal experiments show that nuclear radiation and X-irradiation can increase cancer incidence and mimic aging. Strong doses cause whole-cell destruction, leading to radiation sickness and death. Localized strong doses are used to destroy cancerous cells. All cells are destroyed, but cancer cells are preferentially killed since highly proliferating cells have more rapid DNA synthesis, which in turn are more vulnerable to attack by radiation. Lesser doses do damage indirectly by creating free radicals and disrupting lysosomal membranes. This damage is greater than one would expect by considering only the initial energy absorption. The numerous lysosomal enzymes unleashed do extensive damage.

Cancer can be due to radiation-altered DNA, to radiation-caused free-radical alteration of DNA, to radiation-damaged membranes or to radiation-caused free-radical damaged membranes. The absorption of the initial radiation or the neutralization of the resultant free radical would prevent the damage that leads to malignancy. Many antioxidants are excellent radiation protectors as well as good free-radical scavengers.

This is fortunate. The several proposed mechanisms of cancer development all have the same preventive measure. If all of the proposed causes are correct or even if only one is correct, the preventive device of adequate antioxidant nutrients would be effective against cancer.

I believe that all of these mechanisms are possible. I also believe that natural antioxidants such as vitamin E, selenium and vitamin C will protect against these disease pathways—provided there is a balanced diet and only a minimal exposure to the carcinogens. These sources of cancer sometimes exceed the protective ability of the antioxidants and initiate precancerous cells. Still, a healthy body can prevent cancer even at this stage. We have the immune system as protection.

Immunity

Dr. R. P. Tengerdy, of Colorado State University at Fort Collins, has found that vitamin E significantly increased the resistance of mice and chickens to bacterial infection by enhancing the number of antibody-forming cells, elevating IgG and IgM antibody titers, and stimulating phagocytosis (the elimination of foreign matter by phagocyte cells).[12]

Previously, I have discussed the protective action of vitamin E in terms of its antioxidant and free-radical scavenging activity. However, a Russian report adds another possible mechanism.[13]

Sodium selenite with vitamin E produced higher antibody titers in response to typhoid vaccine than either alone or without both. Selenium alone had some effect, but vitamin E alone had no effect.

Others have confirmed that vitamin E and selenium together increase the body's production of antibodies to various invaders. Thus without vitamin E, the body cannot defend itself as well against carcinogens or wild cells; with extra vitamin E, the body better resists the invaders.[14]

Vitamin E Helps Anticancer Drugs

As mentioned at the beginning of this chapter, National Cancer Institute scientists have found that vitamin E lessens the harmful effects of the widely used anti-cancer drug Adriamycin.

Dr. William McGuire reported at the 1977 meeting of the American Association for Cancer Research that vitamin E protected normal tissue without diminishing the drug's activity against cancer.

Adriamycin is effective against at least ten forms of cancer, according to Dr. McGuire. Unfortunately, a side effect of the drug is deterioration of the heart muscle that may lead to congestive heart failure. This side effect is brought about by free radicals—which vitamin E inactivates.

Summary

Today more and more cancer-causing chemicals are entering the environment. Vitamin E protects us against these cancer-causing chemicals in several ways. The scientific explanations of the various ways are not as important as remembering to get adequate vitamin E in your diet, along with its helpers—vitamins A and C and the mineral selenium.

References

1. Shamberger, Raymond. *J. Natl. Cancer Inst.*, 48:5, 1491-1497, 1972.

2. Jaffe, S. *Exptl. Med Surgery*, 4:278-282, 1946.

3. Epstein, S. S. *Life Sciences*, 972-978, 1967.

4. Wattenberg, Lee W. *J. Natl. Cancer Inst.*, 48:1425-1431, 1972.

5. Wan-Bang Lo, S. and Black, S. *Nature*, 1322, 21-28 December 1973.

6. Franklyn, Robert, *Lancet*, 12 June 1976.

7. Pearce, M. L. and Dayton, S. *Lancet*, 1: 464-467, 1971.

8. Yang, S. P.; Sproat, Harry; Felkner, Cecil; and Castro, Carmen. American Cancer Society meeting, Chicago, 1977; also *Chemical and Engineering News*, 5 September 1977.

9. Rothman, Sara and Broitman, Selwyn. *Modern Medicine*, p. 29, 15 June 1977.

10. Shamberger, Raymond. *J. Natl. Cancer Inst.* 48:5, 1491-1497, 1972.

11. Harman, Denham. Paper given at the annual meeting of the Gerontological Society, 1972.

12. Tengerdy, R. P. International Symposium on tocopherol, oxygen and bio-membranes.

13. Berenshtein, T. F. *Zdrafookhr. Beloruss.* 18:10, 34-36, 1977.

14. Shute, Wilfrid E. *The Complete, Updated Vitamin E Book*, New Canaan, Connecticut: Keats Publishing, 1975.

1983 UPDATE

Vitamins E and C both block the formation of cancer-causing nitrosamines; however, together they are more effective than is either alone. Nitrosamine levels in body fluids are markedly reduced by vitamins E and C (Bruce, W. R., and P. W. Dione, *Am. J. Clin. Nutr.* 33(11), 2511–2513, Nov. 1980).

Ip has shown that vitamin E deficiency increases the risk of cancer development, especially when coupled with a high-polyunsaturated fat diet (Ip, C., *Carcinogenesis* 3 (12) 1453–1456, 1982).

CHAPTER 11

The Surprise of Selenium

THE most exciting news in nutrition in the last ten years has been the realization of the importance of the micro-trace element selenium. Selenium helps protect us from cancer, heart disease and premature aging.

I have been fascinated with this amazing mineral for many years. In 1969 I applied for patents, and in 1970 I filed an Investigational New Drug application (RF929I) with the Food and Drug Administration for drugs that contained selenium.* My laboratory research had shown that selenium was a key ingredient in formulations that prevented cancer from being induced in my laboratory animals by chemicals known to cause cancer, and increased the lifespan of mice in other tests by slowing the aging process.

Several other researchers had been pioneering selenium research. Thanks to the efforts of Drs. Ray-

---

* (Partial listing of selenium patents) Australia, 29107; Belgium, 767, 442; Canada, 142, 747; Denmark, 2432; France, 71-18380, 73-27942; Germany, P2124972.9, P2336176; Great Britain, 16047, 34785; Mexico, 127400, 145062; Netherlands, 71.06929; New Zealand, 163, 719; Sweden, 652071; United States, 39140, 97011, 271655, 398596, 481788.

mond Shamberger, Gerhard Schrauzer, Al Tappel, M. C. Scott, Orville Levander, Doug Frost, Klaus Schwarz, and a small handful of others, the incidence of cancer might well be reduced to only one-eighth or even one-tenth of the present rate.

The incidence of spontaneous breast cancer in susceptible female mice was reduced from 82 percent to 10 percent by Dr. Gerhard Schrauzer of the University of California at San Diego in 1974 merely by adding traces of selenium to their drinking water.[1]

Besides the eight-fold reduced incidence of cancer in Dr. Schrauzer's study, it is important to note that even among the 10 percent of the selenium-supplemented mice that did develop cancer, the disease did not appear until 50 percent later than among the control animals, the tumors were "less malignant," and the control animals' survival time was 50 percent longer. In a less cancer-prone strain of mice, the breast cancer may have been totally prevented. Many studies have led to a growing conviction about the importance of selenium in preventing and controlling cancer.

Dr. Schrauzer is quoted by Richard Stiller in an article scheduled to appear in a mid-1978 issue of *Family Circle*. "We now think that if a breast cancer patient has especially low selenium blood levels, her tendency to develop metastases is increased, her possibility for survival is diminished, and her outlook in general is poorer than if she has normal levels. The key to cancer prevention lies in assuring the adequate intake of selenium, as well as of other essential trace elements."

In 1969, Dr. Raymond Shamberger of the Cleveland Clinic and Dr. Doug Frost of Battleboro, Vermont, noticed an inverse relationship between the incidence of cancer and the amount of selenium in patients' blood samples, and interesting to note, there were the same inverse relationships when the amount of selenium in locally grown crops was considered. The lower the level of selenium, the higher the incidence of cancer.[2]

In 1971, this inverse relationship was found to correlate also with the level of selenium in local cow's milk.[3]

The disappearance of sheep cancer in the part of New Zealand that introduced selenium in anthelmintic drenches for sheep was noted in 1972.[4]

Let's look at some of the epidemiological data. Rapid City, South Dakota, has the lowest cancer rate of any city in one survey in the United States. The citizens of Rapid City also have the highest measured blood selenium levels. But in Lima, Ohio, which has twice the cancer rate of Rapid City, the citizens have only 60 percent of the blood selenium levels of those in Rapid City. Check the inverse correlation between selenium level and cancer death rate in table 11.1.

Table 11.1

SELENIUM CONCENTRATION IN HUMAN BLOOD AND HUMAN CANCER DEATH RATE IN VARIOUS CITIES 1962–1966

City	Blood Se. mcg 100 mi	Cancer deaths per 100,000
Rapid City, S.D.	25.6	94.0
Cheyenne, Wyo.	23.4	104.0
Spokane, Wash.	23.0	179.0
Fargo, N.D.	21.7	142.0
Little Rock, Ark.	20.1	176.0
Phoenix, Ariz.	19.7	126.7
Meridian, Miss.	19.5	125.0
Missoula, Mont.	19.4	174.0
El Paso, Tex.	19.2	119.0
Jacksonville, Fla.	18.8	199.0
Red Bluff, Calif. (Tehama Co.)	18.2	176.0
Geneva, N.Y.	18.2	172.0
Billings, Mont.	18.0	138.0
Montpelier, Vt. (Wash. Co.)	18.0	164.0

Lubbock, Tex.	17.8	115.0
Lafayette, La.	17.6	145.0
Canandaigua, N.Y. (Ontario Co.)	17.6	168.0
Muncie, Ind.	15.8	169.0
Lima, Ohio	15.7	188.0

Raymond Shamberger and C. E. Willis.
CRC Reviews, June 1971

In another study, Drs. Shamberger and Willis found healthy persons between the ages of fifty and seventy-one to average 21.7 micrograms of selenium per 100 milliliters of blood, whereas cancer patients of the same age range averaged only 16.2 microliters per 100 milliliters. The worst cancer cases had the lowest selenium levels (13.7, 13.9, and 14.3).[5]

Table 11.2 shows the inverse correlation with the level of selenium in local crops with the incidence of breast cancer.

Table 11.2

SELENIUM IN CROPS AND
BREAST CANCER RATE

Selenium Crop Concentration, ppm	Breast Cancer Rate Compared to National Average
0.03	11 percent above average
0.05	9 percent above average
0.10	20 percent below average
0.26	20 percent below average

After Raymond Shamberger and Douglas Frost.
Canadian Medical Journal, 100:682, 1969.

The 3 May 1976 issue of *Chemical and Engineering News* added more information about the protective effect of selenium against breast cancer:

The association between high selenium levels in the diet and a lower-than-average cancer rate was suggested in a paper delivered by Dr. Christine S. Wilson, a nutritionist at the University of California, San Francisco. She told the FASEB meeting that high selenium levels in the diet may explain why the breast cancer rate is substantially lower in Asian women than in women from western countries.

After comparing the nutrient content of an average nonwestern diet supplying 2500 calories to that of a typical American diet providing the same number of calories, Wilson determined that the western diets contained about a fourth of the selenium that the Asian diets did. She says that it is also significant that the Asian diets contained much less "easily oxidizable" polyunsaturated fats (7.5 to 8.7 grams a day) than the western diets did (10 to 30 grams).

The University of California nutritionist hypothesizes that it is the dietary combination of high selenium and low polyunsaturated fatty acids that may be protecting the Asian women against breast cancer. She notes that selenium is a component of the glutathione peroxidase system. Because the enzyme acts to inhibit the oxidation of the unsaturated fats, it blocks the formation of peroxides and free radicals, both of which are believed to trigger various forms of cancers. The connection between low cancer rate and high selenium diet was also reinforced by Shamberger, who says that another Cleveland Clinic survey suggests that high selenium levels appear to be associated with a corresponding decrease in deaths from cancer of the colon.

In Venezuela, the death rate from cancer of the large intestine is 3.06 per 100,000 while in the United States it is 13.69 per 100,000. Venezuela has a high selenium content in its soils, while we are low. Japan, another high-selenium country, not only has less breast cancer as already mentioned, but also has a lower lung cancer death rate—12.64 per 100,000 compared to our 36.86 per 100,000.

Further Evidence

The evidence that selenium protects against cancer is even stronger than suggested until now. So far we have considered that extra selenium has reduced spontaneous cancer in mice, and epidemiological studies associate low selenium levels with increased incidence of cancer.

Dr. Shamberger has also shown that painting selenium on the skin of mice near areas that had been painted with the carcinogen DMBA reduced the number of tumors normally obtained with DMBA in the absence of selenium. The selenium was neither mixed with nor painted on the same spot as the DMBA.

In one series of such nondietary experiments, the incidence of tumors dropped from 43 percent with the nonselenium-treated mice to 17 percent with the selenium-treated mice. A second part of the nondietary experiment involved different timing of the selenium application, and the incidence dropped from 89 percent in the controls to 45 percent among the selenium-treated.

In still another nondietary series, this time using the carcinogen MCA instead of DMBA, the incidence dropped from 87 percent in the controls to 68 percent in the selenium-treated mice.

In another series of experiments, the selenium was added in the diet rather than being painted on the skin. This more nearly approximates environmental exposure to carcinogens being contained by dietary supplementation than the "painted" tests.

Dr. Shamberger tested several timing schedules for beginning the diet supplementation after painting the carcinogen on the skin of the mice. The two-week delay experiment described typical results.

In one experiment comparing a selenium-fortified

diet to a selenium-deficient diet against DMBA-croton oil, fourteen of thirty-five mice on the selenium-fortified diet had tumors after twenty weeks, compared to twenty-six of thirty-six mice on the selenium-deficient diet. Those mice on the selenium-fortified diet that did get tumors took longer to develop them.   •

A similar experiment with the carcinogen benzopyrene showed thirty-one of thirty-six mice on a selenium-deficient diet developing cancer, opposed to only sixteen of thirty-six mice on the selenium-fortified diet.[6]

Dietary Carcinogens

To more nearly simulate the problem of ingesting carcinogens in food or water, carcinogens can be added to the diet, and comparisons made between normal diets and selenium-fortified diets. This has been done by Drs. C. G. Clayton and C. A. Baumann with azo dyes,[7] by Dr. J. R. Harr et al. with FAA (1972),[8] and by myself with DMBA (1969-1972). Dr. Lee Wattenberg has done similar experiments with other antioxidants besides selenium.[9]

My experiments were conducted with several antioxidants used in synergistic combination to provide animal protection at the lowest total dosage of antioxidants possible. The incidence of stomach cancer to be expected in mice given DMBA is 85 to 90 percent. That can be reduced to 5 to 15 percent with mixtures of water- and fat-soluble natural and synthetic antioxidants, including selenium.

In my experiments, the mice were given one dose of the carcinogen. They had been raised from weaning on the experimental diets and they continued to receive the same diets after being fed the DMBA.

Dr. Harr's group fed the animals the FAA continually as a part of their diet, during the entire experiment. Various amounts of selenium were also added to the diet thus fed concomitantly with the carcinogen.

They used groups of twenty mice. Group one received 150 ppm FAA and 2.5 ppm added selenium; group two received 150 ppm FAA and 0.5 ppm added selenium; group three received 150 ppm FAA and 0.1 ppm added selenium; and group four received 150 ppm FAA and no added selenium.

After 210 days, 80 percent of groups three and four had cancer, compared to 10 percent of group two and 3 percent of group one. The selenium had a definite protective effect.

At a February 1978 conference on preventing cancer, held at the National Cancer Institute in Bethesda, Maryland, considerable emphasis was given to the role of selenium in preventing cancer. In addition to the updates on the research conducted by Drs. Shamberger and Schrauzer, Dr. A. Clark Griffin, of the M.D. Anderson Hospital and Tumor Institute in Houston, reported that selenium added to drinking water, or selenium fed in the form of high-selenium yeast, can protect rats exposed to three different kinds of cancer-causing chemicals from colon and liver cancer. Dr. Griffin's group has also shown that selenium can prevent the conversion of potentially cancer-causing chemicals into other harmful forms. Experiments by Dr. Charles R. Shaw, also of M.D. Anderson Hospital, show that selenium cuts the bowel cancer rate from 87 percent down to 40 percent in animals fed carcinogens.

Human Chromosomes

Animal experiments have to be used before human clinical trials can begin. This was seen with the elaborate groundwork required to test vitamin A's protective role in human bladder cancer. Until human trials are approved, we have to rely on animal studies and test-tube studies using human cell cultures.

Dr. Shamberger's group investigated the protection of selenium to human chromosomes exposed to carcinogens. They found that the carcinogens did cause chromosomal breaks, and that selenium reduced this damage by 42 percent, vitamin E reduced the damage by 63 percent, and vitamin C reduced the damage by 32 percent.

Mechanisms

How does selenium protect the body from cancer? In several ways; these include its inactivation of free radicals, antioxidant protection of cell membranes (already discussed in earlier chapters), and also detoxification and the stimulation of the immune response.

In the preceding chapter, I mentioned that vitamin E and selenium together were synergistic in stimulating the immune response. Dr. T. F. Berenshtein of the Vitebsk Medical Institute, USSR, reported in 1972 that vitamin E and selenium together before or during immunization showed higher antibody titers than with a vaccine alone. Selenium given alone was less effective in stimulating antibody formation, and vitamin E had no effect on this antibody formation.[10]

In 1976, Dr. John Martin of Colorado State University and Dr. Julian E. Spallholz of the Veterans Administration Hospital of Long Beach, California, reported similar results. They found that dietary selenium significantly increased antibody production. Vitamin E and selenium together enhanced both the primary and secondary immune response. A seven-fold increase in antibodies resulted from 0.7 ppm selenium, and a thirty-fold increase resulted from 2.8 ppm selenium.[11]

Conclusion

Selenium in excess, like vitamin A, is toxic. Dietary selenium content varies regionally. But, since we are not sure of the source of each food item, it seems suicidal not to take 50 to 100 micrograms of selenium supplements daily in this day of high carcinogen exposure. Taking selenium supplements is especially important since the dietary selenium appears to be decreasing, and selenium is protective against cancer and heart disease. I agree with Dr. Schrauzer when he said that if every woman in America began taking selenium today, within a few years the breast cancer rate would decline.[12] But I'll go one step further and say that all cancer would decline.

References

1. Schrauzer, Gerhard. *Annals Clin. Lab. Science*, 4:6, 441-447, 1974. Symposium on Selenium-Tellurium in the Environment, University of Notre Dame, Notre Dame, Indiana, 11 May 1976.

2. Shamberger, Raymond and Frost, Douglas. *Canad. Med. Ass. J.*, 100:682, 1969.

3. Shamberger, Raymond and Willis, C. E. *Crit. Rev. Clin. Lab. Sci.*, 2:211-221, 1971.

4. Wedderburn, J. F. *New Zealand Vet J.*, 20:56, 1972. Frost, Douglas. *Toxicology*, p. 469, October 1972.

5. Shamberger, Raymond and Willis, C. E. *J. National Cancer Inst.*, 44:931, 1970.

6. Shamberger, Raymond J. *Biochem. J.*, 111:375, 1969; *J. Nat. Cancer Inst.*, 44:931, 1970. Shamberger, Raymond J. and Rudolph, G. *Experientia*, 22:116, 1966; *Nature*, 213:617, 1967.

7. Clayton, C. G. and Baumann, C. A. *Cancer Research*, 9:575-582, 1949.

8. Harr, J. R.; Exon, J. H.; Whanger, P. N. and Weswig, P. H. *Clin. Toxicol.*, 5:2, 187-194, 1972.

9. Wattenberg, Lee W. *J. Nat. Cancer Inst.*, 48:1425-1431, 1972.

10. Berenshtein, T. F. *Zdravookhr. Beloruss.*, 18:10, 34-36, 1972.

11. Martin, John and Spallholz, Julian E. Symposium on Selenium-Tellurium in the Environment, University of Notre Dame, Notre Dame, Indiana, 12 May 1976.

12. Quoted by Eric Mishara, *National Enquirer*, 14 April 1978.

1983 UPDATE

Selenium now ranks first in our arsenal against cancer. Not only have there been several new studies confirming the work presented here, but there have been other studies showing additional ways in which selenium is protective.

As discussed in my book *Selenium as Food & Medicine* (Keats Publishing, New Canaan, CT, 1980), selenium has also been used successfully to treat cancer. At this writing, Dr. R. Donaldson of the St. Louis Veterans Administration Hospital is reporting the updated results of his 140-patient study to the National Cancer Institute (May 9, 1983). Some of the patients deemed terminal with only weeks to live are now completely free of all signs of cancer after 4 years. Not all patients were cured, but all had reduction in tumor size and pain. It is unfortunate that they did not receive the selenium until they were pronounced incurable.

Researchers should read *Selenium in Biology and Medicine*, Eds. Spallholz, Martin & Ganther, AVI Press, Westport, CT, 1981).

Papers of interest include:

Nigro et al., *J. Natl. Cancer Inst.* 69:103–7 (1982).
Watrach et al., *Cancer Lett.* 15:137–43 (1982).
Vernie et al., *Cancer Lett.* 14:303–8 (1981).
Ip et al., *Cancer Lett.* 14:101–7 (1981).
Ip et al., *Carcinogenesis* 2(9) (1981).
Gunby, P. *J. Amer. Med. Assoc.* 246:1510 (1981).
Ip et al., *Cancer Res.* 41:31–4 (1981).
Balansky & Argirova, *Experientia* 37:1194–5 (1981).
Soullier et al., *Cancer Lett.* 12:343–8 (1981).
Greeder & Milner, *Science* 209:825–6 (1980).
Medina & Shepherd, *Cancer Lett.* 8:241–5 (1980).

CHAPTER 12

The B-Complex

IN the preceding chapters, I have shown that vitamins A and E and the mineral selenium help prevent cancer and that vitamin C has a role in controlling and offering protection from cancer. The B-complex vitamins play their role as well. They have been researched less than the other vitamins, but they should not be ignored—nor should any nutrient, since they are all important links in the chain of defense and good health.

The B-complex plays an important role in increasing appetite (which suffers in cancer patients), preventing depression and helping to detoxify drugs.

These vitamins offer protection against cancer primarily by their detoxification of cancer-causing chemicals, maintenance of oxygen metabolism and stimulation of the immune response.

The B-complex is largely used in the body as components of enzymes and coenzymes. Thus they are important building blocks of the compounds that control the chemical reactions of life. These reactions include those that get rid of unwanted chemicals by breaking them down, a step at a time, to smaller and simpler compounds until they can finally be excreted.

The body is continually assaulted by many pollutants that can cause cancer. Most of these cancer-causing pollutants can be detoxified by enzymes called Aryl Hydrocarbon Hydroxylases (AHH) and their coenzyme, NADH. NADH is made from niacinamide (vitamin B-3) and is involved in many oxidation reactions in the body.

Oxidation reactions are important in normal cell health. Dr. Otto Warburg long ago noted that normal cells use oxygen-based reactions as their source of energy, and that cells not supplied with adequate oxygen must switch to a lower-energy system based on glucose for their survival. This conversion produces a cancer cell. In other words, normal cells use oxygen, cancer cells don't. Cancer cells thrive on glucose, but are killed by oxygen. Thus the B-complex vitamins may play a role in preventing a normal cell from switching to a cancer cell by maintaining a proper oxygen-fueled energy system. In 1970, Dr. Warburg demonstrated that a vitamin B-1 deficiency would start the cancerous process in cells.[1] In 1947, Dr. R. W. Engel showed that fourteen of eighteen choline (a B vitamin)-deficient rats got cancer, whereas none of the choline-supplemented rats did. In 1966, Dr. Warburg told a meeting of Nobel Prize winners that a plentiful supply of niacin (B-3), riboflavin (B-2), and pantothenic acid (B-5) is the best possible protection against cancer.

Dr. Warburg believed in keeping adequate oxygen in the blood. Daily exercising, vitamin E and B-15 are helpful. Particularly helpful, he felt, were long hot baths—as hot as one can stand. This improves circulation and brings more oxygen to more cells. Long hot baths have been long considered good for the health in Japan.

Pangamic Acid

Pangamic acid, the chemical name for vitamin B-15 (found in seeds, liver, yeast and bran), especially increases the body's efficiency in using oxygen at the cellular level. Thus cells need less oxygen than when they are deficient in pangamic acid, and more oxygen can remain in the bloodstream. Both of these actions increase the oxygen in the cellular environment, thus discouraging normal cells from switching to cancer cells.

Pangamic acid also supplies the body with needed "methyl groups" that can be used in the liver to detoxify many pollutants. Pangamic acid also helps keep the liver healthy by preventing fat-infiltration damage when the liver is overly bombarded with pollutants or alcohol.

The stimulation of the immune response by pangamic acid was demonstrated in guinea pigs and rabbits by the Russian researcher, Dr. G. A. Nizametdinova, in 1972.[2]

TABLE 12.1

SOME NATURAL SOURCES OF PANGAMATE
(MILLIGRAMS PER 100 GRAMS OF FOOD)

Rice bran	200	Wheat bran	31
Corn grits	150	Barley grits	12
Oat grits	106	Wheat flour	10
Wheat germ	70		

After Teleydy-Kovats et al, 1970

Experimental Evidence

Dr. Carlton Fredericks's new book, *Breast Cancer: A Nutritional Approach*, discusses a study at McGill

Medical School involving two groups of women, matched in age, with one group suffering from uterine cancer and the other group essentially healthy.

> "A very large majority of the cancer patients displayed high levels of estrogen, *low intake of vitamin B, and low blood levels of the vitamin*. By coincidence, exactly the same percentage (94.5 percent) of the healthy patients *had high intake of vitamin B, high blood levels* [of the vitamin], and normal or low levels of estrogen" (italics added).

Dr. Fredericks has observed that breast cancer and uterine cancer seem to be related to estrogen level, and that the B-complex vitamins help the liver regulate the estrogen level.[3]

The problems of estrogen use have been discussed earlier. Perhaps this is an oversimplification of Dr. Fredericks's observations, but he stresses the need for the B-complex and high-quality protein to aid the liver in converting estrogen to the less active estriol, a normal process. Dr. Fredericks also notes that "vitamin B-complex added to a diet of hospital-food scraps sharply reduced the incidence of cancer in animals," and that brewer's yeast (a rich source of the vitamin B-complex) lowered the cancer-producing potential of a commonly used food dye.

The Liver

The liver is the body's detoxifying organ. A healthy liver will help keep pollutants at a low level. Good nutrition and health habits help keep the liver healthy. Pangamic acid helps to protect the liver. Some researchers have found that liver extracts from animals injected into other animals have slowed the cancer process. Of particular interest are liver components called cytochrome P-450 and retine which are believed to have strong anticancer properties.

Some cancer patients seem to have particularly damaged or sluggish livers. Some "unorthodox" therapies, such as the Gerson therapy, attempt to relieve a congested liver with the help of coffee enemas.

This sounded strange to me at one time, but I have followed it closely for over a decade, and I believe it has considerable merit. Mae West and V. E. Irons speak warmly of the value of periodic coffee colon irrigation.

Anyone interested in the use of coffee colonics should consult books particularly by Dr. Max Gerson.[4] Check with your physician. Basically a colonic consists of taking an enema of coffee prepared by boiling three teaspoons of ground coffee in a quart of water for ten to twenty minutes and allowing it to cool.

Liver Supplements

An ideal source of nutrients for your liver, of course, is animal liver. Animal livers contain all the nutrients your liver needs. Unfortunately, the components cytochrome P-450 and retine are proteins, and are thus broken down during digestion.

Liver is a great food; it may even contain undiscovered nutrients. Liver extracts alone enhance the endurance of swimming rats, an effect that has not been produced by any combination of known nutrients. Cancer patients would do well to include one-quarter pound of liver (or one ounce of dessicated liver) in their daily diet.

What about the pollutants that may be concentrated in the liver—especially DES or DDT in beef liver? The danger is less in defatted liver because the pollutants are fat-soluble and hence stored in fat.

Also, the liver is the detoxifying organ. Unless the

animal has been grossly polluted, the liver would have already destroyed most of the pollutants.

Yeast, another rich source of the vitamin B-complex, has also been shown to be protective against carcinogen-induced cancer—but this may be due to traces of selenium in the yeast.

References

1. Warburg, Otto. *Z. Naturforsch*, 25:3, 332-333, 1970.
2. Nizametdinova, G. A. *Uch. Zap Kazan, Vet. Inst.*, 112:100-104, 1972.
3. Fredericks, Carlton. *Breast Cancer: A Nutritional Approach*. New York: Grosset & Dunlap, 1977.
4. Gerson, Max. *A Cancer Therapy*. Delmar, California: Totality Press, 1958.

1983 UPDATE

Pangamic acid now goes by its more scientific name, dimethylglycine (DMG). It was never shown to have true vitamin activity, only to act as a metabolic enhancer. DMG has been shown to stimulate two branches of the immune system.[1] This is a major finding.

DMG is essentially non-toxic and is not a carcinogen or a mutagen, despite an erroneous report to the contrary.[2]

1. Graber, C.D., et al, *Journal of Infectious Diseases* 143(1) 101–105 (1981).

2. Loveday, K.S. and Seixas, G.M., Bioassay Systems Corp. Report No. 10261. No evidence of mutagenicity by DMG either alone or after incubation with nitrite or saliva (March 27, 1981).

Also see

Passwater, R.A.; The Truth about DMG, *Bestways* 10(2) 72–77 (1982).

Bolton, S. and Null, G. Vitamin B15 Review and Update, *J. Orthomol. Psy.* 11(4) 260–266 (1982)

CHAPTER 13

Laetrile:
Does it Work?

I delayed writing this book for two years awaiting the scientific answer to whether or not Laetrile aids in the control of cancer. For two years, both sides of the Laetrile debate did little to settle the issue. Both sides were dogmatic and argued with emotion rather than with facts.

However, what little evidence was produced seemed definitely to indicate that Laetrile has its place in cancer therapy. It has not been *proven* that Laetrile aids in cancer control; but neither has it been proven that Laetrile does *not* aid the cancer patient. I wish I knew more facts about Laetrile, but they have yet to be presented in a manner in which the scientific community can make a sound judgment.

I have talked with many respected physicians in several countries, including one who became a U.S. Congressman. These all believe that Laetrile therapy produces a rapid noticeable improvement in nearly all cancer patients, and produces significant improvement or remission in 10 to 30 percent of those patients with solid tumors. However, most of these physicians also administer supernutrition (megavitamin therapy) simultaneously and can't honestly say that the Laetrile was a key ingredient in the therapy.

I have also talked with many cancer patients who believe that the Laetrile was a crucial part of their therapy. Several claim that when they discontinue Laetrile, their tumors return; when they reinstate the Laetrile, their tumors begin shrinking again.

Anecdotal evidence is not scientific evidence, but one cannot help but be influenced by the many dramatic "cures" told by so many former cancer sufferers. They were in pain and despair, and are now happy to have health again. Some have had remissions for longer than ten and twelve years.

These claims can no longer be ignored. It is time for government-sponsored research to test Laetrile in willing cancer patients under scientifically controlled conditions. Such a test may have to be forced by a class action suit. I want my tax money spent on seeking the truth, not on the propagation of bureaucratic opinions.

Part of the problem is that Laetrile is not a patented drug owned by a pharmaceutical firm that has the resources to provide the documentation required for approval by the FDA. And how many drug firms would have sales of their current offerings for cancer treatment damaged if a simple nutrient such as Laetrile proves to be effective? And how much influence on federal agencies and elective officials does the drug industry have? Then there is the NIH syndrome—"Not Invented Here"—in the scientific community. If one can't get credit for developing Laetrile, why pursue it? That's no way to a Nobel Prize or peer esteem.

The Laetrile picture has been clouded with emotional issues such as freedom of choice in medical therapy versus protection of the masses by a well-meaning, paternalistic bureaucracy.

Recent Evidence

Let's look at the recent evidence about Laetrile before discussing the basic facts about the nutrient.

In September 1977, Dr. Harold W. Manner, chairman of the Department of Biology of Loyola University in Chicago, announced that Laetrile, in combination with vitamin A and pancreatic enzymes, produced a nearly 100 percent cure of breast cancer in mice.[1]

Dr. Manner and his colleagues used 105 mice that had developed breast cancer in his experiment. He left twenty-one mice untreated to serve as experimental controls. The tumors in the control group continued to grow during the eight-week experiment.

Eighty-four mice were treated with Laetrile, vitamin A and enzymes. Complete regression of the mammary tumors occurred in seventy-five of the mice, and partial regression occurred in the remaining nine mice during the eight weeks.

The combination produced results that Laetrile alone did not achieve. At this writing, Dr. Manner is expanding his experiment to see the effectiveness of all possible combinations of the three substances.

Dr. Manner felt it was necessary to present his evidence directly to the public because, as he pointed out, "I'm not a youngster in science. I'm fifty-two years old and I've always gone to journals in the past. But in this case I don't think we've got that kind of time. Going through the normal channels could mean a delay of eighteen months or more."

Dr. Manner believes the action of Laetrile is very similar to that postulated by Dr. Ernst Krebs, but with important differences. "The tremendous amounts of the unlocking enzyme, b-glucosidase, present in tumor cells free cyanide from Laetrile, and there isn't enough of the inactivating enzyme, rhodanese, to inactivate it. But it isn't an all or none reaction in cancer cells as Dr. Krebs proposed. All cells have both enzymes, but tumors have much higher concentrations of the unlocking enzyme." Dr. Krebs postulated that normal cells produced rhodanese and cancer cells produced b-glucosidase.

Earlier, Dr. Manner had published results proving that Laetrile is nontoxic.[2]

He commented on Laetrile's safety in *The Choice* in September 1977. "In the Mexican clinics the cancer patients are getting up to a dozen grams of Laetrile injected into them daily. Our lab mice were given the equivalent of 210 grams a day for fifteen days and we didn't lose a mouse.[3]

"In fact, the animals receiving Laetrile looked far better than those receiving the placebos. The experimental mice had shinier hair, brighter eyes and more energy."

Israeli Results

Some dramatic results were achieved during 1977 in Israel. Ten cancer patients received 70-gram-per-day injections. Dr. David Rubin of the Israeli Medical Research Foundation, Ltd., Jerusalem, says that breast cancer reacts best to Laetrile treatment, and that the large doses also have a good effect on bone cancer. He has had no success with leukemia.

Dr. Rubin is using Laetrile alone without other nutritional therapy. According to *The Choice*, Dr. Rubin became interested in Laetrile after his mother's impressive response to Laetrile for her breast cancer.[4]

Prior to Dr. Rubin's own clinical tests, he visited several Laetrile clinics. On September 1, 1976, he submitted a report to the Ministry of Health of Israel. The following is his summary:

1) With few exceptions, all of the cases we saw were advanced incurable cancer patients. Most of them had had conventional therapy before being treated with Laetrile.

2) The most striking observable feature was relief of pain accompanied by a decrease or even cessation of the need for pain killers and sleeping potions. It is interesting to note that in the majority of cases the patients came off long-term use of narcotics without the usual withdrawal symptoms.

3) After a few days of treatment with Laetrile there was an improvement in appetite followed, in many cases, by a gain in weight.

4) A frequent striking feature in cancer wards is the odor of decaying cancer masses. We observed that this fetor is generally absent in the cases of patients under Laetrile therapy.

5) Laetrile is nontoxic to normal somatic cells and may be given by injection in doses up to 5 grams per kilogram of patient weight per day.

6) There is no contraindication to giving Laetrile in addition to orthodox therapies such as surgery, toxic chemotherapy and hormones.

7) In general, it is claimed that the Laetrile patients experience a sense of well being and the quality of their life improves with the important result that the patients regain hope that their disease will be brought under control with consequent extension of their lives without undue discomfort and without the need for mind-clouding narcotics as previously required. In very many cases it appears from our preliminary observations that this is indeed what takes place.

In short, it is our conclusion that: a) Contrary to many allegations in both the scientific and lay literature, Laetrile is not quackery; b) Laetrile is non-toxic even in very large injected doses; c) Laetrile has a definite palliative effect. We cannot, at this stage of our investigations, say that it inhibits tumors but the evidence we have suggests that it does. We must do controlled studies to rule out the possibility that prior therapies had some effect on the tumors that stopped growing. However we doubt that the regressions we observed were due to the "delayed effects" of other therapies because, in our experience, such delayed effects rarely, if ever, occur.

Animal Studies

Studies have shown an almost 100 percent inhibition of cancer by apricot kernels alone in a strain of mice particularly susceptible to breast cancer.

In March 1977, I had the opportunity to address the Environmental Matters Committee of the Maryland House of Representatives in Annapolis. Also addressing the House Committee that day was Dr. Vern L. van Breemen of Salisbury State College, Maryland, who told the legislature: "About a year ago, I set up an experiment with two special strains of mice . . . one which spontaneously produces mammary carcinomas [breast cancer] and another which spontaneously develops leukemia.

"This is a pilot experiment to compare the occurrence of leukemia and tumors in mice fed the usual diet supplemented with apricot kernels.

"So far, seven animals in the control group have died of leukemia and five have died with the mammary carcinoma. None has died from these diseases in the apricot kernel-fed animals. This is a significant difference."

In the August 1977 issue of the *The Choice*, Dr. van Breemen reported that one of the apricot kernel-fed mice developed a "slowly growing" tumor but otherwise exhibited good health for "an old mouse." Dr. van Breemen also reported that the results were not as dramatic in the leukemic mice, but those eating the apricot kernels were undergoing life extensions of up to 50 percent over what normally would be expected.[5]

Dr. van Breemen's research findings are in agreement with Dr. P. G. Reitnauer's findings at the Manfred von Ardenne Institute in Germany in 1973.[6] Dr. Reitnauer inoculated mice with cancer cells (Ehrlich ascites carcinoma). The controls were fed regular lab diets, while others were also given bitter almonds. Compared with the control group, the bitter almonds resulted in prolongation of survival and inhibition of tumor growth.

Several studies have been made at the Memorial Sloan-Kettering Cancer Center with mixed results. Researchers at the center seem to be in disagreement as to what is expected of a compound to fight cancer and how to test for it.

I attach more importance to naturally occurring tumors in mice rather than to tumors transplanted to regions, such as their tails, where the blood circulation is poor. Also, I am more concerned with the general health and longevity of the animal than I am with its tumor size. Some researchers do not consider the lifespan of the mouse, but only whether or not the tumor shrinks. I know several healthy people who regained their health first; then, months later, their tumors began shrinking. I also know of several people who have had their tumors shrunk by chemotherapy, but suffered such ill health and weakened immune response that they died of pneumonia during treatment.

Nicholas Wade reported the problems of overzealous overkill among one group of scientists at Sloan-Kettering Institute in his article "Laetrile at Sloan-Kettering: A Question of Ambiguity."[7]

"The Institute's first problem occurred when Dr. Kanematsu Sugiura, the scientist put in charge of Laetrile testing, got what might, in one perspective, be called the 'wrong' results. He found that Laetrile tended to inhibit the growth of secondary tumors in mice, although it did not destroy the primary tumors. Dr. Sugiura did the experiment three times, again with the same outcome.

"Sugiura, now eighty-five, is an emeritus member of the Sloan-Kettering and his abilities are held in high regard. . . . He has had more experience in tumor testing than anyone at the institute. . . . and he has an extraordinary record through the years of being right.

"Sugiura's first group of experiments was completed in 1973 but was not published in the usual way. Asked about the departure from customary scientific practice, Stock [Chester Stock, vice-president for Chemotherapy Research at Sloan-Kettering] explains that 'If we had published those early positive data, it would have caused all kind of havoc.' Good [Robert Good, Head of Sloan-Kettering] adds that 'the natural processes of science are just not possible in this kind of pressure cooker'."

In opposition to Dr. Sugiura's findings, Laetrile, under selected experimental conditions, was tested in fourteen animal tumor systems, with no significant anticancer activity. But what is significant? Did the animals do better on Laetrile? Or are the scientists merely observing that the tumors did not shrink immediately? What doses were used? Was pain reduced? The questions arise because, although the apparent negative results were widely distributed to the media in a large press conference on June 15, 1977, they were not scheduled to be published for scrutiny until mid-1978 in the *Journal of Surgical Oncology*.

Remember, Edison did not have success with the light bulb until after one hundred experiments. A few quick experiments do not usually uncover enough information to optimize experimental conditions, let alone offer proof of a negative occurrence.

Nicholas Wade went on in his *Science* article: "Dr. Sugiura's position differs from that of his colleagues. He stands by his original findings, which he has repeated in the same [experimental] system, and with similar results in two other systems. He continues to believe that Laetrile is not a cure for cancer but is a palliative agent."

In Dr. Sugiura's report, he states that his opinion is based on his own observations in his experiments, "which include inhibition of lung metastases (secondary tumors), temporary initial stoppage of growth of small primaries, inhibition of the appearance of new tumors, and the better health and appearance of treated mice."

It has been pointed out by a group at Sloan-Kettering, calling themselves "Second Opinion," that the report presented to the press omitted other positive findings of Laetrile's effectiveness. A three-experiment series by Dr. Franz Schmid found Laetrile ineffective in two of the experiments; but there was a positive anti-tumor effect in the third experiment which was statistically significant. Yet Sloan-Kettering told the media that "all experiments of three independent observers . . . have failed to confirm Sugiura's initial results."

The Second Opinion group charged that the negative tests bore little resemblance to Dr. Sugiura's experiments. As an example, Dr. Schmid used a very small dosage of Laetrile compared to Dr. Sugiura's dosage.

Still in the negative tests, the Laetrile-treated mice lived longer—in one test, 50 percent longer—than the "control" mice. Of course they developed more cancer in those two tests! The longer-lived, Laetrile-treated mice had more opportunity for the cancer to spread. Perhaps the higher dosage suggested by Dr. Sugiura would have completely stopped the cancer spread, as well as kept the animals in better health longer.

Another experiment conducted by Dr. Daniel Martin of the Catholic Medical Center in Queens, N.Y., was equally flawed. Dr. Martin administered Laetrile only to the forty-sixth day of treatment, as opposed to Dr. Sugiura's method of giving daily injections for life. Laetrile proponents have always contended that Laetrile therapy is not a "one shot deal," and like vitamins, must be taken daily.

The Second Opinion group also pointed out, based on Dr. Sugiura's memos, that once Dr. Sugiura visited Dr. Martin's laboratories in the summer of 1976, and because Dr. Sugiura could readily distinguish visually which mice were receiving Laetrile and which were receiving saline solution (salt water), Dr. Martin terminated the experiment. Dr. Sugiura could easily tell which mice were receiving Laetrile, because they were the healthier mice. However, Dr. Martin claimed that Dr. Sugiura had broken the code that insures the "blindness" of the study, and thus the experiment was then invalid.

The experiment that was terminated by Dr. Martin was begun anew at Sloan-Kettering's Walker Laboratory in the fall of 1976. However, a most questionable maneuver was made in an attempt to prevent the code from being broken. The mice were mixed up in the cages at random. Their ears were notched in a code which was supposed to inform the technicians which "shot" to give which mouse. Some of the shots were Laetrile and others were saline solution.

Ear notches become difficult to interpret over a period of time, and since many mice have to be treated every day, the chances for error are huge. Dr. Sugiura warned them of this in several memos, and he was right again. The mice did get mixed up—or you will have to believe that salt water—which has never cured cancer before—cured 40 percent of the mice in this test. Yet Sloan-Kettering reported this exercise in futility as evidence that Laetrile doesn't work.

The Second Opinion group also pointed out that the

files of Dr. Elisabeth Stockert contain a preliminary experiment showing a positive anticancer effect of Laetrile. Second Opinion also noted that *Laetrile had been tested primarily in a system* (CD_8F_1 spontaneous mammary cancer) *in which no other agent is effective.*

That is what you do when you want to fail. It is like trying to find out if someone is strong by asking him to lift a million pounds.

The charges by Second Opinion are valid. They have been substantiated by several scientists—including *Science*'s Nicholas Wade, who calls the errors of presentation "a serious flaw."

Dr. Stock has since admitted that none of the eight drugs is effective in that strain of mice in the experimental conditions under which Laetrile was tested.[8]

On 18 November 1977, the New York *Post* carried a bold headline, "Sloan-Kettering Docs Rap Own Laetrile Report," which told of the assistant Public Affairs director at Sloan-Kettering, Dr. Ralph Moss, joining the pro-Laetrile group. "He said he had been sent by the center to respond to the dissident group but felt he 'could not do so honestly,'—and joined them instead.

" 'We don't know if Laetrile does work,' Moss said. 'We don't claim this report is proof that Laetrile works. All that we are asking is that Laetrile be tested fairly, adequately and completely.' "

This is in essence what I requested of the FDA in my testimony to them on 1 March 1977 (Docket # 77N-0048). That testimony, in large part, follows.

"I submit the following testimony to show that there is no valid reason to impound, ban or remove Laetrile (laevo-mandelonitrile-beta-glucoside) from interstate commerce, or to restrict the physician from prescribing this nutrient in his practice. Further, I offer testimony to illustrate that the Food and Drug Administration's present policy on Laetrile is counterproductive to the

Administration's own objectives concerning this nutrient.

"Also, the Food, Drug and Cosmetic Act of 1962 does not apply to Laetrile because the nutrient was in safe and effective use as a cancer control compound in interstate commerce before 1962. The Administration's press release P77-8 of February 17, 1977, states that Laetrile has been promoted as a cancer cure for about twenty-five years.

"Perhaps the first documented successful use of Laetrile for cancer control was in December 1951 by Arthur T. Harris, M.D., of Los Angeles, as reported in *Laetrile—Control for Cancer* by Glenn D. Kittler.[9] Many hundreds of documented successful applications have resulted since then, both nationally and internationally.

"Therefore, it must be concluded that by virtue of its marketing before the 1962 Food, Drug and Cosmetic Act, Laetrile is exempt from the law's requirement that a drug be shown by scientific evidence (double-blind studies) to be safe and effective before it can be marketed. The 'grandfather' clause is the basis for the exemption.

"The question of safety is one more reason that the Administration should discontinue its present policy. All compounds, including water, can be misused to be harmful to the body. Laetrile has been shown to be completely nontoxic when used under the guidance of qualified physicians. Laetrile is a natural nutrient and a member of a family of water-soluble nutrients classified as B-complex nutrients.

"Laetrile is less toxic than many nutrients that are in our daily food supply—and much safer than many drugs. The cyano group ($C\equiv N$) of vitamin B-12 (cyanocobalamin) is more labile and potentially more harmful than the cyano group found in Laetrile. Yet we know how safe and essential vitamin B-12 is.

"The Administration must realize the danger in driving Laetrile underground and removing it from the hands of qualified physicians is to have it used by the unqualified layman who is unaware of safe usage or effective usage ranges. Propaganda by the Administration that Laetrile is toxic is counterproductive to proper usage. Instead, warnings should be issued not to allow large quantities of Laetrile or natural seeds brew for long periods of time in acid media, which degrades Laetrile, thereby producing the toxic cyanide ion.

"Additionally, the Administration should be concerned with product purity and assay. This function is of great value to the people the Administration is chartered by Congress to serve.

"The Administration repeatedly claims that scientists have never found any evidence to support the theories regarding how Laetrile works. (Press Release P77-8, 17 February 1977.) This is a poor argument to deprive those in agony from the proper usage of Laetrile.

"It has only been recently that we have learned of the prostaglandin mechanism through which aspirin works. (I am having difficulty locating double-blind studies of aspirin. Could it be that aspirin should be banned? After all, we know it is harmful to all in large doses and deadly to a few at low dosages).

"Recently, Dr. Keith Brewer and I proposed a mechanism through which we believe that Laetrile works as published in the *American Laboratory*, April 1976. If our theory is correct, then it is only reasonable that evidence has not been found to verify the older theories. The question to be addressed is not whether theories can be substantiated but whether it works to control some types of cancers in a number of individuals.

"Many of the tests attempting to examine the question of effectiveness have serious experimental flaws unknown to the researcher. As an example, if our theory is correct, these experiments in which tumors were transplanted to rat tails could not have been expected to work due to an inadequate blood supply in the rat tail.

"If the researcher doesn't fully understand the mechanism involved, an improper experiment can result. A negative finding from such an experiment cannot be taken as proof that Laetrile doesn't work—especially in the light of empirical evidence from the real world—actual cancer patients—that Laetrile does indeed work to relieve pain, control tumor growth and even cure cancers of various types.

"The fact that not all cancers respond to Laetrile therapy can be better understood with the theory presented by Dr. Brewer and me. In essence, the theory is as follows:

"The attachment of cancer-causing agents (carcinogens) to cell membranes eliminates the transport of oxygen across the membranes. A drop in the hydrogen ion concentration (pH) level from 7.35 to 6.0 follows, due to the conversion of glucose into lactic acid as a consequence of the elimination of oxygen. Lysosomal enzymes are liberated, and nucleic and amino acids are fermented within the cell as a consequence of the foregoing. The reaction of lactic acid and lysosomal enzymes with cell DNA to destroy the normal DNA-RNA (genetic) reactions and control mechanism of the cell follows.

"The indicated therapy then is to raise the pH level to 9 which theoretically can be accomplished in those having low pH tumors with a suitable nitrile (Laetrile) which will enzymatically yield the cyano group ($C\equiv N$) within the cell.

"The consequence of the absorption of the cyano group on and in the cell membrane is that it will materially enhance the permeability of the membrane for cations through potassium in the electromotive series and also depresses the electronic excitation of the membrane's phospho ($P=0$) groups.

"The presence of CN groups on the cell membrane will materially enhance the transport of potassium ions into the cell. Since only a fraction of these ions are essociated with glucose under normal conditions, the net result is that the increased accumulation of these strongly electropositive cations within the cell will tend to raise the pH of the cytoplasm. In fact, when sufficient cyano groups are on the membrane surface, the possibility exists that the cell will become appreciably alkaline provided there are sufficient potassium or especially rubidium ions in the contact fluid. This fact may be most significant in cancer therapy. Laetrile may be one part of the control, while potassium or rubidium may also be required for another part. Laetrile alone is not as effective as with other therapies.

"Rather than slamming a door in the face of the public on the Laetrile issue, the Administration should be actively pursuing qualified experts to conduct laboratory and clinical experiments to test Laetrile under various conditions, against various cancers and according to various theories. It is obvious that pharmaceutical firms are not interested because Laetrile cannot be patented by them.

"It is also noted that the Administration stresses in its press release P77-8 of 17 February 1977 that 'despite intensive effort over many years, the FDA, the American Medical Association, the American Cancer Society, the National Cancer Institute and independent researchers have been unable to find any scientific evidence that Laetrile has any effect on cancer.'

"This position is definitely erroneous. It is true, of course, that Laetrile has not 'dissolved' all malignant tumors. However, it has stopped the spread (metastases) of cancer in controlled tests at the Memorial Sloan-Kettering Cancer Center in New York in tests conducted by Dr. Kanematsu Sugiura from 1973 to 1975, involving six different studies. Thus it has shown antineoplastic activity. A second test at Sloan-Kettering did not confirm the first test results due to difference in the material used. A third series of tests confirmed the effectiveness of Laetrile.

"It is important that effectiveness be measured in several ways—not just the reduction of tumor size which does not indicate the overall health of the host. Survival time, reduction of pain and metastases should be a more accurate measure of cancer control.

"Perhaps the Administration has based its judgment on tumor size alone. A smaller tumor, and critically ill host is not as good as a same-sized tumor, but well host. Even in the Sloan-Kettering second report that did not confirm the first, there was a 55 percent increase in survival time.

"Other studies have found Laetrile or its food sources to be effective. Successful tests have been conducted at the Southern Research Institute in 1973 (Birmingham), Manfred von Ardenne Research Institute in 1973 (Dresden), and Scind Laboratories of the University of San Francisco in 1968. The physicians of many countries are successfully using Laetrile as evidenced by many thousands of testimonial letters of its benefit.

"Another point that the Administration ignores is the constructive influence of the mind over illness. Today the physician must tell the terminal cancer patient there is nothing else that can be done. The patient is sent home to die without any hope. This aspect often increases morbidity and mortality. It would be better if the physician would treat the patient with Laetrile and megadoses of vitamins and say 'Let's see if this works.'

"If Laetrile was proven to be only a placebo, a placebo in the hands of a physician can indeed work miracles. So can prayer. When the Administration takes away placebos, it is essentially the same as taking away hope and prayer.

"Was this the intention of Congress when they chartered the FDA?

"Finally, the Administration should recognize that their present policy has failed to discourage the public from wanting and using Laetrile. You have only succeeded in forcing people underground and making model citizens in the agony of cancer commit criminal acts of smuggling. You have forced the price upward due to the risks of smuggling, making it unnecessarily expensive to the stricken. You are inviting organized crime in an area that belongs to organized medicine.

"What do we know of the quality and purity of material smuggled in from foreign countries?

"The argument that Laetrile doesn't work has been judged poor by the public, resulting in a severe erosion of public confidence in the FDA. The policy is viewed as a scientific Watergate or Swine Flu vaccination program. The public knows that it has been lied to by officialdom, and experts have been wrong about Swine Flu, Red Dye No. 2 and a host of other controversies. The public believes that coffee, oil and gas shortages have been shown to be somewhat manipulated.

"The current inflexible and outdated stand by the Administration is not only judged to be in error by the public, but is believed to be contrived by the Administration to protect former erroneous decisions, at the expense of those now in agony. A frequent question raised is who is the FDA supposed to be protecting—the public or past decisions? And, at what price is the protection from what evil?

"This also raises the question of benefit-to-risk considerations. The only risks involved seem to be (1) misuse and (2) avoidance of conventional therapies. Both risks can be avoided by placing Laetrile in the hands of qualified physicians free of restrictions from the FDA and medical societies. However, the Administration must recognize the constitutional right of freedom of choice in therapy by the patient.

"The FDA should refrain from harassing Laetrile proponents and calling its use quackery. Conventional therapies are far from perfect and can use all of the help possible.

"Drs. James E. Enstrom and Donald F. Austin of the University of California School of Public Health and Tumor Registry reported in *Science* (4 March 1977) that 'both the age-adjusted total cancer incidence rate and the age-adjusted total cancer mortality rate changed by only a few percent between 1950 and 1970 . . . the fact that neither has changed significantly since 1950 implies that the total cancer survival rate has also remained essentially constant.'[10]

"Since we need better therapies, we must examine the question if the past decision of a benevolent administrator outweighs thousands of favorable reports from the real world. We need to reexamine the issue periodically to prevent strategies from being out of phase with realism. The time is here for Laetrile.

"In summary, malfeasance on behalf of the Administration has taken a safe nutrient that aids in the control of cancer out of the hands of physicians and caused citizens suffering from cancer to smuggle Laetrile into the country.

"I have presented herein evidence that Laetrile is exempt from the Food, Drug and Cosmetic Act of 1962, and is a safe and effective agent in the control of cancer. There is no valid reason for prohibiting interstate commerce of Laetrile or harassing physicians prescribing it.

"I suggest that FDA should consider letting physicians use Laetrile and correlate the results much in the manner of a New Drug Application. Let us move together to aid those in the agony of cancer now so that our conscience will be clear the remainder of our lives."

After hearing testimony from the FDA and many concerned citizens, in December 1977 Federal Judge Luther Bohanon of Oklahoma City ordered the Federal Government immediately to cease interfering with the importation, introduction, delivery or use of Laetrile. In addition, Judge Bohanon ordered the Government to refrain from interfering with any licensed medical practitioner administering Laetrile.

Judge Bohanon ruled, "By denying the right to use a nontoxic substance in connection with one's own personal health care, FDA has offended the constitutional right of privacy." He also ruled "FDA has not established that Laetrile is a 'new drug' that it can declare illegal, because the drug has been commercially sold and used in the United States for more than twenty-five years."

The judge ordered the FDA's ban on Laetrile to be "set aside and vacated" because such a ban is "arbitrary, capricious . . . an abuse of discretion, and is not in accordance with law."

Many people trying to save their lives or lives of their loved ones had been convicted as criminals, and physicians arrested and stripped of their licenses to practice medicine because of the FDA's ban, which Judge Bohanon ruled unlawful in itself.

Background

Laetrile is being used in twenty-eight countries. Physicians outside the United States strongly advocating the use of Laetrile include Dr. Hans Nieper, Director of the Department of Medicine at the Silbersee Hospital in Hanover, West Germany, Dr. N. R. Bouziane, Director of Research Laboratories at St. Jeanne d'Arc

Hospital in Montreal, Canada, Dr. Ernesto Contreras of the Good Samaritan Cancer Clinic in Tijuana, Mexico, Dr. Manvel Navarro, Professor of Medicine and Surgery at the University of Santo Tomas in Manilla, the Philippines, Dr. G. Maisin of the University of Louvain, Belgium, D. Ellore Guidetti of the University of Turin, Italy, and Dr. Shigeaki Sakai (private practice) of Tokyo, Japan.

In the United States, battles have been fought on behalf of Laetrile by Dr. John Richardson of Albany, California, Dr. James Privitera, West Covina, California, Dr. Stewart Jones of Palo Alto, California, Dr. Arthur Harris of Los Angeles, California, Dr. John A. Morrone of Jersey Medical Center in Jersey City, New Jersey, and others.

What makes these physicians fight for their right to use Laetrile to help their patients? Stupidity? Boredom? Wanting to make a fast buck? I doubt it; it would be easier to do a mass practice with Medicare patients or needless surgery. I can only conclude that they have had greater success with Laetrile therapy than with conventional therapy or have grown impatient with the limited success of conventional therapy.

What Is Laetrile?

Laetrile is also known as amygdalin or vitamin B-17. Laetrile is a shortened form of the chemical name LAEvomandeloniTRILE-beta-glucoside, or mandelonitrile glucuronide, a nitriloside. Chemically, it can be thought of as molecules of benzaldehyde, hydrogen cyanide and glucuronic acid all linked together to form a molecule having different properties than its components. However, when the unlocking enzyme, beta-glucosidase reacts with Laetrile, the molecule is broken down to release the cyanide which kills the cancer cells. Cancer cells are killed because the enzyme beta-glucosidase is present in large quantities only in tumors, therefore, appreciable quantities of cyanide are released only within cancer cells. Additionally, normal cells contain plenty of an inactivating enzyme, rhodanese, which converts cyanide to thiocyanate, which does not kill cells and is excreted harmlessly.

Natural Sources

The following list of natural sources of Laetrile was published by *Choice* in November 1975.

KERNELS OR SEEDS OF FRUIT (highest concentration of vitamin B-17 to be found in nature aside from bitter almonds): Apple, apricot, cherry, nectarine, peach, pear, plum, prune.

BEANS: broad. (Vicia faba), burma, chick peas, lentils (sprouted), lima, mung (sprouted), Rangoon, scarlet runner.

NUTS: bitter almond, macadamia.

BERRIES (almost all wild berries): blackberry, chokeberry, Christmas berry, cranberry, elderberry, rawberry, strawberry.

SEEDS: chia, flax, sesame.

GRASSES: acacia alfalfa (sprouted), aquatic, Johnson, milkweed, Sudan, tunus, velvet, wheat grass, white clover.

GRAINS: oat groats, barley, brown rice, buckwheat groats, chia, flax, millet, rye, vetch, wheat berries.

MISCELLANEOUS: bamboo shoots, fuschia plant, sorghum, wild hydrangea, yew tree (needles, fresh leaves).

Mike Culbert, in his outstanding book *Freedom from Cancer*, gives guidelines for eating Laetrile-containing foods. He also cautions the reader that anything in excess is dangerous. His first rule is to eat all fruits whole (seeds included) and not to eat more seeds alone than normally eaten in whole fruit.[11]

Mike Culbert's second rule is to eat one peach or apricot kernel per ten pounds of body weight.

That nitrilosides such as Laetrile might prevent or control cancer is suggested by the fact that a territory whose inhabitants are reportedly cancer-free eat a diet rich in Laetrile. Hunza, a principality in the Gilgit Agency in Pakistan-controlled Kashmir, bordering China, Afghanistan and India, has been confirmed to be cancer-free by UNESCO. The 40,000 Hunzakuts lead an ordered, relaxed, relatively stress-free life, eating vitamin-rich foods, keeping busy with manual labor and dancing. They have inbred for centuries and have been protected from outsiders by the Hindukush mountain range, the Pamirs and the Yarkand River Valley. Their air is pure. They see few synthetic chemicals, let alone food additives, pesticides and chemical fertilizers. Their soil is rich in selenium and rubidium. Apricots are their prime crop; they eat the fruit and nuts and use apricot oil for cooking. They are free from western medicine and are believed to have the longest lifespans on this planet. It's no wonder they are cancer-free.

Laetrile Pioneer

Dr. Ernst Krebs, Jr. of San Francisco is generally credited for pioneering the use of Laetrile against cancer. He pieced together the bits and pieces of information and synthesized the substance which he called vitamin B-17 until he named it Laetrile. Research has indicated that Laetrile is the same substance as amygdalin, which had also been used in cancer therapy in France and Germany in 1865.[12] Dr. Krebs, his late father (who died cancerfree at age 93) and brother Byron have been the instrumental forces bringing Laetrile to its present status. Of course, those who believe that Laetrile has helped control their cancer have really been the ones who have brought about the legalization of Laetrile in thirteen states at this writing.

Safety

Safety is of vital concern. Earlier in this chapter, I have quoted researchers and physicians as saying Laetrile is essentially nontoxic. This is not to say that its use is not without danger. Laetrile should only be used under medical supervision. To attempt to treat yourself for cancer is pure folly. Laetrile therapy and all nutritional therapies discussed in this book are compatible with conventional therapies, and should be administered by physicians trained in their use. Organizations that can supply lists of such physicians are given in the final chapter.

The FDA is assigned the task of guaranteeing the safety and purity of drugs. Unless Laetrile is legalized, people will smuggle in Laetrile of unknown purity or go to other countries for treatments. I would rather have the FDA inspect and certify the purity and strength of Laetrile for use in this country wherever it is legalized.

Contamination of the injectable drug can cause severe fever or even death. This is true for any injectable substance. Dr. Philip S. Schein, Chief of the Georgetown University's Medical Oncology Division in Washington D.C., thought he had uncovered two cases of adverse reactions from the drug. Dr. Schein and his Georgetown colleagues alerted the medical profession, and the public via press conferences, of the two cases allegedly badly affected by impure Laetrile.

However, one of the two patients involved, Carol M. Dunn of Washington, D.C., responded with a letter to the Editor of the Washington *Post Magazine*.[13]

As the biased article on Laetrile in the September 4 issue discusses my "allergic reaction" to Laetrile, although it does not mention my name, I would appreciate an opportunity to express my views.

1) I personally do not consider the reaction as serious. As a nurse, I have seen more severe reactions in patients allergic to aspirin or penicillin.

2) My worst and most severe reaction (if it was a reaction to Laetrile) came more than twenty-four hours after having taken Laetrile. Also, I had been taking it in large doses for over three months.

3) I have had worse reactions to chemotherapy and radiation. Have also seen even more severe reactions.

4) The majority take Laetrile as a last resort—after the doctors have given extensive radiation and chemotherapy—and have given up.

5) Cases that were given up by the Mayo Clinic have had complete repression of all symptoms after taking Laetrile.

6) I turned to Laetrile when I had to give up an experimental drug which had kept my condition under control for years. A drug I can no longer obtain because the National Cancer Institute is now experimenting with the drug on animals. Previously, I was told it was not effective on animals.

7) While on Laetrile, my blood remained fairly stable. When I resorted to chemotherapy my red blood count dropped from twenty-eight to twenty-three. My platelets also dropped severely.

8) Chemotherapy did not reduce my enlarged lymph nodes.

9) No doubt, more people have died while taking chemotherapy and radiation than Laetrile.

> 10) At the present time I have a choice of taking full-body radiation, which can cause cancer in other parts of the body, or chemotherapy which will cause nausea, vomiting, bone marrow depression, loss of hair, anemia, etc.

No wonder more people are turning to Laetrile!

Toxicity is still possible in improper use of tablets or injectable. One of the most toxic of all drugs is the drug 5-FU (5-Fluorouracil) often used in chemotherapy. This drug has a narrow margin of safety even in the healthiest of patients.

In August 1977, Dr. Julius Richmond, assistant secretary for Health (Surgeon General), warned, "As our experiences with Laetrile grow, we are finding that it is not harmless. Quite to the contrary, we are finding that Laetrile is a dangerous substance, especially in its oral form." He reported thirty-seven documented cases of poisoning and seventeen deaths, allegedly from Laetrile. He also warned, "We are increasingly receiving reports from physicians of patients with early, curable cancer who have turned to Laetrile and then found out too late that it does not work." He urged cancer patients to avoid "this dangerous, fraudulent drug."

Certain foods may free the cyanide from Laetrile under certain conditions. Thus if cyanide is released in food mixtures or the stomach, it will poison the nervous system and possibly cause immediate death. The release of cyanide can be catalyzed by enzymes in almonds, celery, peaches, lettuce, bean sprouts, alfalfa sprouts and some others under certain conditions as suggested below. The danger would be greater in critically ill patients with impaired respiratory systems.

Dr. Eric S. Schmidt and his colleagues at the University of California at Davis blended almonds with Laetrile in a paste and *incubated* them. They fed the incubated mixture to dogs who showed definite signs of cyanide poisoning. Although humans would not consume such foods incubated with Laetrile, the experiment draws attention to a possible hazard.[14]

It is obvious that there are widely differing opinions on whether Laetrile helps control cancer and whether Laetrile has serious toxicity.

Since there seems to be no protective rights to the compound that would warrant anyone's underwriting the millions of dollars of tests required to resolve the issue, I believe the Government should do the testing. It should use total nutrition therapy along with whatever conventional therapy it would normally use. Animal studies will not resolve the issue of pain reduction and improved well-being. People who would take Laetrile anyway should volunteer for the tests. These volunteers should not be given placebos as controls in place of Laetrile.

If the Government does not take the responsibility for the human testing, it may well be contributing to needless suffering and death. As citizens we should exert all the pressure possible to force the proper authorities to take action.

References

1. Manner, Harold W. Lecture at the National Health Federation Regional Meeting, Chicago, September 1977. *Choice*, 3:8, 16-19, 1977. *National Health Federation Bulletin*, 23:10, 1-3, November 1977.

2. —————— *Science of Biology Journal*, May/June 1977.

3. —————— *Choice*, September 1977.

4. Rubin, David. *Choice*, 3:6, 8-9, July 1977.

5. Breemen, Vern L. van. *Choice*, August 1977.

6. Reitnauer, P. G. *Arch. Geschwulstforsch*, 42:2, 135-137, 1973.

7. Wade, Nicholas. *Science*, 23 December 1977.

8. Nelson, Harry. *Los Angeles Times*, P. 1, 15 January 1978.

9. Kittler, Glenn D. *Laetrile Control for Cancer*. New York: Paperback Library, 1963.

10. Enstrom, ames E. and Austin, Donald F. *Science*, 4 March 1977.

11. Culbert, Michael L. *Freedom from Cancer*. New York: Pocket Books, 1977.

12. Inosemtzeff, T. *Gaz. Med Paris*, vol. 13, 1845. Wodinsky, I. and Swiriarski, J. K. *Cancer Chem. Reports*, 59:5, 939-950, 1975. Halstead, Bruce W. *Amygdalin (Laetrile) Therapy*. Los Altos, California: Choice Publications.

13. Dunn, Carol M. *Washington Post Magazine*, 16 October 1977.

14. Schmidt, Eric S. *et al*. JAMA, 239:943, 6 March 1978.

1983 UPDATE

Laetrile still presents a confusing picture, as convincing data is lacking. However, the anti-laetrile group has done more verifiable studies than the pro-laetrile group. I have not witnessed a groundswell of laetrile-cured cancer patients, despite the legalization of laetrile in many states. I have not seen any published studies in the scientific or medical literature indicating that laetrile is effective.

The anti-laetrile group has published a clinical trial, but it is of questionable value because it was run on terminally ill persons who were not helped by any other therapy (Moertel, C.G. et al., *New Eng. J. Med.* 306(4):201–207, Jan. 1982).

The pro-laetrile group has other objections to the study, but they seemed to have these objections well in advance of the study. However, Dr. James Cason of the University of California at Berkeley, has shown by means of infrared spectrophotometry, that the compound used in the Moertel study did not contain amygdalin (laetrile).

CHAPTER 14

Minerals

WE have already discussed the major role the mineral selenium has in preventing cancer. Other minerals also play important roles, although not as well established.

In 1974, Dr. Hans A. Nieper, Director, Silbersee Hospital in Hanover, Germany, told the second annual convention of the Cancer Control Society, "We run whole blood analyses by the thousands. What is most interesting is that all patients who have malignancies, even in beginning stages and even in small children, have a very much deteriorated mineral picture."

Is this poor blood mineral content due to poor diet? Is it due to a condition that prevents minerals from being absorbed by the body or carried in the bloodstream, even causing the abnormal use of minerals? We have no answers as yet.

Potassium

A common factor in many of the nutritional therapies for cancer is the inclusion of potassium-rich foods. Sodium-rich foods are decreased, and foods such as leafy green vegetables, whole grains, nuts, potatoes, bananas, oranges and milk are emphasized.

This is a good general health practice especially in terms of heart disease and cancer. My colleague, Dr. A. Keith Brewer, has noted that cancer cells appreciably take up potassium; even more important, he has found that additional potassium increased the alkalinity of the cell, causing cell death.

Dr. Brewer also believes that cancer cells can liberate hydrogen cyanide from nitrilosides such as Laetrile, which becomes attached to the cell membrane and enhances the transport of potassium, cesium and rubidium ions into cancer cells. These strongly electropositive cations will increase the alkalinity of these cancer cells.

Dr. Brewer comments, "It is not surprising that nitrile-eaters such as those found in Bangladesh are essentially immune to cancer. Nitriles in the diet, combined with a high potassium food intake should drastically reduce, if not eliminate, the possibility of cancer. This would especially be true when there is also an appreciable concentration of rubidium in the food intake."[1]

Table 14.1

THE POTASSIUM CONTENT OF FOODS

Milligrams per 100 grams (3.50 ounces) Edible portion	
8060 Dulse (1 tsp. = approximately 242	420 Chicory greens
	414 Mushrooms
5273 Kelp (1 tsp. = milligrams) approximately 160 milligrams)	410 Salmon
	407 Potato with skin
	401 Collard leaves and stems
2927 Blackstrap molasses (1 tsp. = approximately 146 milligrams)	397 Dandelion greens
	397 Fennel
	390 Brussels sprouts
	382 Broccoli
1700 Brewer's yeast, dry	380 Liver, calf's or beef
1495 Rice bran	378 Kale
	377 Mustard greens

1121	Wheat bran	376	Wheat, soft winter
920	Sunflower seeds, hulled	370	Banana
827	Wheat germ	370	Wheat, hard
773	Almonds	369	Winter squash
763	Raisins	355	Ground round, raw
727	Parsley	341	Carrots
725	Sesame seeds, unhulled	341	Celery
714	Rice polish (note that	340	Brains
	rice bran contains	340	Pumpkin
	potassium as rice	335	Beet root
	polish)	320	Chicken, light meat
694	Prunes, dried		without skin, raw
674	Peanuts	310	Beef kidney
648	Dates	310	Persimmon, native
640	Figs, dried	295	Cauliflower
604	Avocados	294	Nectarine
603	Pecans	294	Escarole
600	Yams	282	Watercress
570	Beet greens	281	Apricot, fresh
550	Swiss chard	280	Sweet corn
541	Parsnips	278	Asparagus
540	Halibut	268	Red cabbage
500	Chinese waterchestnuts	264	Lettuce, all types
470	Spinach		except iceberg
467	Rye grain	256	Coconut meat, fresh
464	Cashew nuts	251	Cantaloupe, casaba,
450	English walnuts		honeydew melons
450	Collard leaves	250	Chicken, dark meat
430	Globe artichokes		without skin, raw
430	Millet	249	Okra
244	Tomato	170	Blackberries
243	Sweet potato (compare	168	Red raspberries
	with yams!)	164	Strawberries
243	Snap beans	165	Grapefruit juice, fresh
234	Papaya	160	Beef heart
233	Green cabbage	160	Cucumber
231	Onion, green	158	Grapes, slip skin
220	Wild rice	146	Pineapple
214	Eggplant	141	Lemon juice
214	Brown rice	140	Buttermilk
213	Sweet green peppers	140	Whole cow's milk
202	Peaches, fresh	135	Grapefruit pulp
202	Summer squash	130	Pear, fresh
200	Orange, peeled	126	Tangerine
199	Black raspberries	110	Apple
194	Figs, fresh	102	Chayote
191	Cherries	101	Apple juice
189	Mangoes	100	Eggs, whole
182	Orange juice, fresh	100	Watermelon

180	Goat's milk	92	Wine, unfortified
180	Lobster	82	Cranberries
175	Iceberg lettuce	81	Blueberries
173	Grapes, adherent skin	55	Cooked oatmeal
170	Peas, podded	10	Honey

Composition of Foods, Agriculture Handbook, No. 8, U.S.D.A. 1963.

Iodine

A relationship between breast cancer and iodine deficiency was reported by Dr. Bernard A. Eskin of the Woman's Medical College of Pennsylvania in 1970. Dr. Eskin found that estrogen hastens the development of dysplasia (abnormal tissue development) when iodine is lacking from the diet.[2]

It is important to note that cancer occurs four times as often in dysplastic breasts than normal breasts. However, there is no evidence that benign dysplasia turns into cancer.

A study of the county by county cancer mortality rates from 1950 to 1969 sheds some light on the issue. Although iodized salt had been introduced, cancer has a long latent period.

The highest breast cancer mortality rates are found in states bordering the Great Lakes. All of the significantly high counties were within the iodine-deficient goiter belt, or the New Jersey to Massachusetts strip. Perhaps a combination of iodine deficiency plus carcinogen is required to initiate breast cancer.

The importance of iodine may be related to the thyroid hormone, thyroxine, which governs the rate of metabolism. The rate of metabolism influences the degradation of estrogen into estriol. Estrogen tends to be carcinogenic or at least cocarcinogenic, and low iodine results in having estrogen remaining in the body longer.

Zinc

Zinc seems to help prevent cancer. Zinc plays a very important role because of its role in enzymes—especially the enzymes in the lymphocytes called desaminases.

In the April 1975 issue of the *Journal of the National Cancer Institute*, it was reported that 60 percent of mice injected with sarcoma cancer cells did not develop the usual tumors if they also received 80 milligrams of zinc daily.

Doctors Paul M. Newberne and Y. Y. Fong of the Massachusetts Institute of Technology have shown that zinc deficiency increases susceptibility to esophageal cancer. Esophageal cancer patients have low zinc levels in blood, hair and esophageal tissue. When rats are fed a low-zinc diet and given a tumor-promoting chemical, 79 percent develop tumors, compared to only 29 percent of those on an adequate zinc diet.[3]

Dr. Hans Nieper said, "We know from our experience that as soon as the blood zinc level drops to less than six parts per million (the normal is eight ppm), the immune system becomes impaired. Our auspices so far as zinc is concerned will also concern the behavior of lymphocytes. The more lymphocytes which act against cancer cells, the more safety we have against cancer growth. Zinc orotate greatly activates the development of T-lymphocytes and increases their number, especially when a large amount of vitamin A is given at the same time. Both vitamin A and zinc are essential ingredients the thymus gland needs to inform lymphocytes to fight cancer cells."[4]

Don't forget that zinc is also needed for the absorption of vitamin A. Zinc should therefore be a part of any regimen to prevent or cure cancer.

Other Minerals

All essential vitamins and minerals play a role in the health of the body. Without them, death results. I have only highlighted those nutrients available evidence suggests have direct roles in the prevention and cure of cancer.

Any program to resist cancer must also contain the other nutrients as well as those specifically highlighted. Certainly more information will come in the years ahead that will increase our knowledge about cancer defenses. Until then, a total supernutrition program is essential.

References

1. Brewer, A. Keith. *Amer. Lab.*, 8:4, 37, April 1976.
2. Eskin, Bernard A. Trans. *N. U. Acad. Sci.*, 32:911, December 1970.
3. Newberne, Paul M. and Fong, Y. Y. *Science News*, 113:6, p. 88, 11 February 1978.
4. Nieper, Hans. *Cancer Control Journal*, Vol. 2, No. 5, 1974.

1983 UPDATE

Along with the increased interest in beta-carotene and vitamin A, zinc is also receiving more study. Zinc is required for retinol-binding protein which transports vitamin A throughout the body.[1]

Rubidium is not an essential trace element, but it may have a role in mineral transport across defective cell membranes such as those occurring in cancer. My laboratory studies have shown that rubidium decreased the numbers of tumors and average tumor weight in laboratory animals fed carcinogens or receiving transplanted tumors.[2]

1. Brewer, A.K. and Passwater, R.A., *Amer. Lab* 8(4):80 (1976).

2. Brewer, A.K. et al., *Cytobios* 24:99–101 (1979).

Part Three
BLUEPRINT AND GAME PLAN

CHAPTER 15

Vitamin A

VITAMIN A (Retinal or Retinol) is a fat-soluble vitamin with known toxicity. The provitamin A, carotene, is found in plants and is converted in the body to vitamin A. Carotene comes from vegetable sources such as carrots, peas, lettuce, sweet potatoes, and tomatoes. Retinol comes from animal sources such as liver, eggs and dairy foods.

Functions of Vitamin A

Growth—If adequate vitamin A is not provided for normal growth, bone growth halts and the brain becomes overcrowded in the skull, resulting in paralysis and blindness in severe cases.

Epithelial Tissue Health—The skin epidermis and mucous membranes are made up of epithelial cells. Vitamin A deficiency causes an abnormal condition in epithelial tissues, such as dry flaky skin and mucous membranes that do not secrete mucous normally and are less resistant to disease.

Xerophthalmia—Vitamin A deficiency causes an eye condition where the tear glands cease to function, the eye becomes dry and the cornea (another epithelial tissue) becomes dry and ulcerated. Blindness can result.

Nightblindness—Visual pigments are a combination of vitamin A plus a protein. Rhodopsin is a vitamin A-containing pigment in the light receptors called "rods" and iodopsin is the vitamin A-containing pigment in light receptors called "cones."

After stimulation by light, a chemical change occurs so the body must resynthesize the visual pigments, wherein some vitamin A is lost in the process. Without sufficient vitamin A reserves, night blindness—the inability to see in dim light—results.

Deficiency Signs

In general, mild deficiency signs include loss of appetite, weakness, susceptibility to diseases of the eyes, ears and kidneys, secondary anemia, kidney stones, cystitis, gastritis, sinusitis and bronchitis.

The following deficiency symptoms have been compiled by Dr. John Marks of Downing College, Cambridge, England.[1]

General—Loss of appetite, inhibited growth, increased susceptibility to infections

Skin—Dry and scaly, poor hair production

Eyes—Nightblindness, xerophthalmia, keratomalacia (softening of the cornea)

Respiratory Tract—Extensive damage of lining cells, loss of ciliary epithelium, multiple infections

Digestive Tract—Damage of mucous membrane, loss of gland activities, poor absorption, infections

Urinary Tract—Metaplasia of epithelium and increased stone formation

Bones—Halting of growth in young. In dogs, overgrowth of porous bone tissue with resulting nerve compression

Reproductive System—Infection of genital tract, degeneration of ovary, decline in fertility

Nutritional Status

In 1969, the U.S. Public Health Service released figures from a 12,000-person, ten-state study of people from all walks of life; 13 percent were deficient in vitamin A, according to RDA standards.

The survey found that 68.5 percent of women over sixty were not getting the RDA of 5,000 I.U. of vitamin A. Fifty percent were not getting even a meager 3,000 I.U. daily, and 40 percent failed to get 2,000 I.U. daily.

Dr. Barbara A. Underwood of Pennsylvania State University reports that as many as 30 percent of the population show below average concentrations of vitamin A in the liver.[2] Low liver stores of vitamin A indicate a long-term vitamin A deficiency.

During periods of prolonged stress or illness, the body can lose up to 60 percent of its vitamin A.

Also, consider that the mineral zinc is required to maintain normal concentrations of vitamin A in the blood where it can become available to the rest of the body. Without adequate zinc intake, the vitamin A will remain in the liver. Pity the health of those deficient in both zinc and vitamin A.

Vitamin E is required to protect vitamin A against oxygen while circulating through lung tissue.

Requirements

The 1974 Recommended Daily Allowances (RDAs) are as follows:

	I.U.
Males, above 11 years of age	5,000
Females, above 11 years of age	4,000
Females, pregnant	5,000
Females, lactating	6,000
Children, 1-3 years of age	2,000
4-6 years of age	2,500
7-10 years of age	3,300
Infants, 0.0-0.5	1,400
0.5-1.0	2,000

However, the RDA is not based on vitamin A's ability to prevent or control cancer at any dosage.

The National Academy of Sciences admits that few experiments have been conducted to determine the minimum daily requirement of human adults, and these have involved few subjects. Since few studies have been conducted on the vitamin A requirement of human infants, the RDA for this age group is deduced from the fact that human milk apparently supplies *adequate* vitamin A for good health during the first year of life. Human milk has a vitamin A content of 170 I.U. per 100 milliliters. Assuming consumption of approximately 850 milliliters (1.8 pints) of human milk per day, the infant would receive about 1,500 I.U. of vitamin A, and this is taken as the RDA.

Investigations are needed to establish the requirements for vitamin A during childhood, adolescence and other periods when growth spurts normally occur. In the absence of such studies, only interpolated estimates of allowances are made for boys and girls, based on average body weights, plus additional arbitrarily decided amounts to satisfy anticipated growth needs.

There is a difference between "adequate" and "optimal." None of the estimates considers cancer prevention.

As Dr. E. Cheraskin and his colleagues at the University of Alabama said in a 1976 article in the *Inter-*

national Journal for Vitamin and Nutrition Research, "The Food and Nutrition Board grants that the RDA has been estimated from dark adaptation (visual) studies, a combination of dark adaptation and blood values, and by extrapolation from lower animal studies. There is no claim that this (RDA) dosage is intended as the ideal daily intake for the maintenance of overall general health."[3]

Dr. Cheraskin's group determined the level of vitamin A which produces the healthiest people. They reasoned that relatively symptomless and sign-free persons are healthier than those with clinical symptoms and signs. Therefore, the intake of such groups might well provide a basis for designating the "ideal" daily vitamin A consumption.

The following conclusion was reached by Dr. Cheraskin's group: "Approximately 33,000 I.U. of vitamin A may be designated as the 'ideal' daily allowance. This is almost seven times the RDA of 5,000 I.U. for the adult male and eight times higher than the 4,000 I.U. RDA for adult females. It is recognized that the 'ideal' is nonexistent as a theoretical end-point since there is biochemical individuality."

I find this sensible approach to be in agreement with my own recommendations published in 1975 in *Supernutrition: Megavitamin Revolution.*

I listed 25,000 to 35,000 I.U. as the dosage range that most people will find as their optimum or Supernutrition level. I pointed out that some individuals will find 10,000 I.U. to be their optimum level, and that a few will find problems at 35,000 I.U., but the majority of people may be in their best health at 25,000 to 35,000 I.U.

I also pointed out that 75,000 I.U. would bring problems to many people with long-term usage, and 200,000 would be toxic to most people.

Toxicity

If you get too much vitamin A, you get some of the same symptoms you would get with vitamin A deficiency, plus a yellowing of the skin and eye whites. The toxicity signs are dry, rough skin, peeling skin, hair loss, yellowing of skin and eye whites, painful joint swellings, nausea, elevated intracranial pressure, dizziness, intense headache, irritability, tension, weakness and stiffness.

Dr. Donald R. Davis of the Clayton Foundation Biochemical Institute of the University of Texas put the benefit-toxicity relationship in perspective in an article scheduled (at the time of this writing) for *Osteopathic Medicine* in mid 1978.[1]

"It seems to be difficult to inform and protect the public without either fostering unrealistic apprehensions on the one hand or ironically and tragically encouraging enthusiasts to believe that *all* apprehensions are unrealistic on the other hand. Two recent editorials, one by a physician who treated two adult cases of toxicity and reviewed the literature, emphasize entirely legitimate concerns about the risks of toxicity and birth defects (very large doses cause birth defects in animals). But when the authors conclude that supplements containing more than 6,000 or 10,000 I.U. should not be sold or used without prescription, they risk losing one of the most important portions of their audience.

"Vitamin A toxicity must rank as one of the most minor of public health or nutritional problems. Less than an average of about five cases of hypervitaminosis A have been reported annually in the U.S., and so far as I have been able to find out, not one has ever proved fatal. (There is a newspaper account of a suicidal death of a Ph.D. chemist in England.) No doubt there are many unreported and undetected cases as well as possible but virtually undetectable cases of birth defects. But the same must be said for a multitude of far more serious problems, including the acute and subtle toxicities of even safe nonprescription drugs. Analgesics alone directly cause tens of thousands of emergency room treatments and hundreds of deaths annually in the U.S., often from therapeutic doses. Another far more serious public health problem may be *inadequate* intakes of vitamin A; about 10 percent of the U.S. population has low or deficient serum levels, and birth defects are a prominent result of inadequacy as well as gross excess in animals.

"While vitamin A toxicity is a minor problem compared to most others, it is hardly minor for those who were hospitalized for weeks or months undergoing tests (and some surgery) prior to correct diagnosis. The fact that the potential toxicity of vitamin A can be exaggerated should not lead enthusiasts to exaggerate its safety."

Dr. Davis then addressed himself to the problem of "How much is safe?"

"This seemingly simple question has no simple or well-founded answer. Suitable prospective experiments have not been done, and because of the risk of birth defects, experiments with large doses cannot be done with women who may conceive. Prolonged doses of only a reported ten to twenty times the recommended dietary allowances have caused serious toxicity in sensitive individuals. These are the individuals who must receive our attention if we are attempting to answer the question for a broad audience interested in taking large amounts for months without monitoring, without specialized knowledge, and for no purpose other than a hope for superior nutrition. Much higher doses may be safe or appropriate for brief periods or for adequately monitored therapeutic purposes.

"Individuals clearly vary greatly (by a factor of ten or more) in their ability to tolerate very large amounts for prolonged periods, and this factor alone makes impossible any simple answer to the question, 'how much is safe?' Another complication is that a relatively unsaturated liver is able to store very large amounts, perhaps 10 million I.U. in adults, or 50,000 I.U. beyond that which can be metabolized daily for 200 days. (Virtually none is excreted except in certain diseases.) Hence amounts which are safe (and perhaps beneficial) for short periods may become toxic after a few months or longer.

"The best available answers to the question posed must be based on a review of the amounts which have been reported to cause serious toxicity. A safety factor of unknown magnitude must be added if we intend to avoid not only serious reactions, but also mild toxicity.

"For infants up to age three, Oliver has published a review of twenty-seven cases reported through 1957. The average reported intake was over 200,000 I.U./day, more than 100 times the RDAs for this age group. A few were as high as 500,000 I.U./day for as long as two years. But the four lowest daily intakes and their durations before onset of serious symptoms were 12,500 I.U. for fourteen months, 30,000 I.U. for six months, 37,500 I.U. for sixteen months, and 50,000 I.U. for eight months. On the basis of this evidence doses of ten to twenty times the usual recommended allowances risk serious toxicity in *sensitive infants* and young children if prolonged more than a few months.

"For adults and adolescents, no suitable review of a sufficient number of cases seems to be available. Accordingly, I reviewed nearly all reports known to me for those of age eighteen or more and included four adolescents ages fourteen to sixteen. A few reports were not readily available, and four cases were excluded for nonexistent or doubtful dose information or for doubtful vitamin A toxicity, leaving twenty-one cases remaining.

"Doses of vitamin A which caused chronic toxicity ranged from a reported 90,000 to 600,000 I.U. daily. The average was 230,000 I.U./day, surprisingly about the same as that for the infants mentioned above. Symptoms reportedly developed after six weeks to eight years, with no reliable relationship to the amounts taken. The lowest daily intakes and their durations before onset of symptoms were 9,000 I.U. for three years, 100,000 I.U. for one year, 100,000 I.U. for three and a half years, and 75,000 to 150,000 I.U. for seven years, followed by several at 15,000 I.U. for four months to four years.

". . . In Europe extremely large doses of vitamin A were used for brief periods in the treatment of cancer and some skin diseases. A special emulsified form of the vitamin (A-Mulsin) is said to initially bypass the liver and to give the greatest therapeutic effect with the most tolerable toxicity. A total of 30 million I.U. is given in gradually increasing doses over about two to three weeks, or longer for much larger doses. 'All patients show a complete desquamation' of the surface skin, and some other typical symptoms occur, including severe headache.

"Although the special emulsion reportedly gives more rapidly rising serum vitamin levels than the usual oily forms of aqueous emulsions (Aquasol), it is unclear whether the special emulsion is significantly different or safer than the usual forms for purposes of prolonged use at moderate dose levels. It may well not be safer. In fact, its toxicity or tolerability, even when taken in huge doses for brief periods, does not seem qualitatively different than those of Aquasol as reported in 1956 by a physician. He experimentally took 15 million I.U. in fourteen days and four months later took 25 million I.U. in twenty-five days without the precautions and drugs used with the special emulsion to control some toxic reactions.

"Even if the special emulsion does have reduced toxicity on a short and possibly long-term basis, its proponents advise against its use for cancer therapy in pregnancy, glaucoma, and liver disease. And for skin diseases which may be controlled with very large doses, they do not use it for long periods except in adults because 'disturbances of bone growth are likely.' In short, very large doses of the vitamin in any form become comparable to a toxic drug which is used carefully in serious conditions where the apparent benefits outweigh the risks.

"Although vitamin A is safe in moderate excess, and its potential toxicity has often been exaggerated, it can be seriously toxic in sensitive individuals if taken in amounts of ten to twenty times the recommended allowances for prolonged periods. Nutrition-conscious professionals and members of the public need to avoid both extremes of apprehension and complacency if they are to seek the potential benefits of improved nutrition without taking the risk associated with drugs and other major public health hazards."

Dr. Eli Seifter, associate professor of Biochemistry and Surgery at the Albert Einstein College of Medicine in New York, discussed vitamin A safety in a recent paper. "Some people worry about the toxic effects of vitamin A overdosage. We think that these fears, although not without foundation, are grossly exaggerated."[5]

Dr. Seifter also pointed out that carotene, the provitamin form of vitamin A found in foods such as carrots and corn, is converted to vitamin A in the body and that no toxic effects are produced from consuming high amounts of carotene. Tests indicate that carotene's effect on the thymus gland and immune system is the same as vitamin A (retinol). Dr. Seifter remarked,

"Those who drink great amounts of carrot juice may find that their skin gets yellow, but other than that there are no toxic effects." This is confirmed by the RDA publication of the National Academy of Sciences.

Sources

Vitamin A-rich foods include the yellow vegetables, liver, cod liver oil, fish oils, butter, cheese, eggs, milk, yellow fruit, and bright green vegetables. Popular sources are carrots, sweet potatoes, chicory, dandelion greens, spinach, turnip greens, liver, whole milk, butter, cheese, egg yolk, corn, bananas and cod liver oil.

The yellow carotene in the green vegetables is masked by the chlorophyll. Some vegetables and fruits deviate from the general color rule. Even though yellow in color, oranges, rutabagas, and yellow wax beans are not good sources of carotene. Other foods containing little vitamin A are nuts, grains, vegetable oils, muscle meats and light-colored fruits and vegetables.

Table 15.1

VITAMIN A VALUE OF SOME TYPICAL FOODS*

Food	Portion	I.U./Portion
Liver, beef, fried	2 oz.	30,280
Potatoes, sweet, baked	1 medium	8,910
Carrots, cooked	0.5 c	7,610
Spinach, cooked	0.5 c	7,290
Kale, cooked	0.5 c	4,070
Mustard greens, cooked	0.5 c	4,060
Apricots, canned	4 med hf	2,120
Broccoli, cooked	0.5 c	1,875
Peaches, raw	1 med	1,320
Eggs, whole	1 med	590
Ice cream, plain	0.25 pt	370

Milk, whole	1 c	350
Cheese, process	1 oz.	350
Orange juice, fresh	0.5 c	245
Butter (average)	1 pat	230
Margarine, fortified	1 pat	230
Bananas	1 med	190
Apples, raw	1 med	50
Pecans	1 tbsp	10
Bread, whole wheat	1 slice	Trace
Oatmeal	0.5 c	0

* U.S. Department of Agriculture

References

1. Marks, John. *The Vitamins in Health and Disease: A Modern Reappraisal*. London: J. and A. Churchill, Ltd., 1968.

2. Maugh, T. H. *Science*. 186:4170, 1198, 1974.

3. Cheraskin, F. et al. *Nutritional Journal for Vitamin and Nutrition Research*, 1976.

4. Davis, Donald R. *Osteopathic Medicine*, mid 1978.

5. Seifter, Eli. 170th Amer. Chem. Soc. Natl. Meeting, Chicago, 29 August 1975.

1983 UPDATE

When deciding how much vitamin A to use as a supplement, be sure to estimate first how much vitamin A and beta-carotene are in your normal diet.

A few individuals may find that 15,000 I.U. of supplemental vitamin A will be too much. Keep in mind that beta-carotene is the preferable source for vitamin A due to its essential non-toxicity.

CHAPTER 16

Vitamin C

VITAMIN C (ascorbic acid or ascorbate) is a water-soluble vitamin with no known toxicity. The medical profession tried for 150 years to ignore the findings of Dr. James Lind of the English Navy that citrus fruits could prevent scurvy. Now there is a tendency to judge vitamin C status merely on the absence of scurvy. Scurvy is a final stage of vitamin C deficiency disease, not an early stage. The anti-scurvy factor was isolated in Hungary by Dr. Albert Szent-Györgyi in 1928, and identified as ascorbic acid in 1933 by him and also by Drs. Waugh and King of the University of Pittsburgh.

Man is one of the few species of animal that cannot make his own vitamin C.

Functions of Vitamin C

All the functions of vitamin C have not been established. Vitamin C is important for the formation and maintenance of the connective tissue protein, collagen, the "ground substance" "cementing" material that holds the cells of the body together. Vitamin C also plays a role in the function of the adrenal gland and the metabolism of the amino acid tyrosine.

Vitamin C is essential for wound healing, the health and integrity of endothelial tissues, the lining of the heart, blood and lymphatic vessels, oxygen metabolism and leucocytic (white blood cell) and phagocytic activity (the destruction of foreign substances).

Vitamin C is a partner with the B-complex in nourishing the thyro-adrenal system, and a partner with vitamin D in regulating calcium metabolism.

Deficiency Signs

Subclinical scurvy is difficult to describe because of its general and nonspecific nature. Some of the symptoms are physical weakness, tendency to bruise and bleed easily, weight loss, shortness of breath, rapid respiration and heart beat, anemia, tooth decay, atrophy of major glands and organs, joint pains and bleeding gums.

Nutritional Status

A 1955 survey conducted by Dr. Agnes F. Morgan of the U.S. Department of Agriculture found 40 percent of American women to be deficient in vitamin C. A 1965 survey found 30 percent of all Americans were deficient in vitamin C according to the RDA standards. In the 1969 U.S. Public Health Service Survey, 15 percent of the population was deficient.

Requirements

The 1974 Recommended Daily Allowances (RDA) are as follows:

Adults (over 11 years)   45 milligrams

Pregnant women	60 milligrams
Lactating women	80 milligrams
Children (1-10 years)	40 milligrams
Infants (0-1)	35 milligrams

The evolution of information on the human requirement for vitamin C has been greatly hampered by lack of knowledge of the role performed by this vitamin. It appears that vitamin C has multiple functions—either as a coenzyme or, possibly, as a cofactor where the rate of reaction is critical.

As with vitamin A, Dr. Cheraskin and his colleagues at the University of Alabama sought to obtain a better measure of vitamin C needs. Again they reasoned that relatively symptomless and sign-free persons are healthier than those with clinical symptoms and signs. They concluded that the intake of such persons might well provide a better guide for daily vitamin C consumption.

They evaluated 1,038 dentists and their wives in terms of their clinical symptomatology and vitamin C consumption. In a progressive selection of healthier subgroups (those with fewer and fewer symptoms and signs), the vitamin C intake increased to 410 milligrams daily in those with no symptoms and signs. This seemed to be a threshold value and no information could be ascertained on higher levels. The 410 milligram threshold is about nine times the RDA.[1]

Disease states might require much higher levels.

I have found that some people reach their supernutrition point (optimum health) at 500–750 milligrams, whereas a few need more than 4000 milligrams.

Toxicity

There is no known toxic effect, although reason tells us there is a safe limit to everything including water. But it looks as though vitamin C is safer than common table salt. Nevertheless, every action has its reaction, so moderation is once again the rule.

Precautions

Cut back dosage if diarrhea occurs. The sodium ascorbate form often found in chewable tablets should not be taken by people on low-salt (low-sodium) diets. People taking anticoagulants or other medication should consult their physicians. Vitamin C is a mild diuretic, but this is not a significant problem.

Preferred Forms

Calcium ascorbate is a mild form well tolerated by most people even at very high dosage. Vitamin C usually utilizes body calcium for its transportation and limited storage. Taking calcium ascorbate supplies this calcium needed by vitamin C, so that body stores are not used. Zinc and magnesium ascorbates are also preferred over ascorbic acid or sodium ascorbate, but all forms are effective.

Comments

Dr. Linus Pauling has caused many researchers to look into vitamin C chemistry. Several others are trying to uncover possible problems with high doses of the vitamin. From time to time suspected problems arise which so far have turned out to be no problems at all. Occasionally we hear that vitamin C does not improve our health or prevent illness. These topics will be touched upon here.

Since Dr. Pauling's book *Vitamin C and the Common Cold* appeared,[2] there have been several controlled trials in which some of the subjects received vitamin C (100 mg or more per day) and others received a placebo over a period of time during which they were exposed to cold viruses in the ordinary way, by contact with other people.

Seven of the studies were well designed, whereas six had experimental flaws. The well-designed tests are summarized in Table 16.1.

Table 16.1

SEVEN SUCCESSFUL VITAMIN C TESTS

Year	Researchers	Percentage Decrease in Illness
1942	Cowan, Diehl, Baker—Minnesota	31
1961	Ritzel—Switzerland	63
1972	Charlestown, Clegg—Scotland	58
1973	Anderson, Reid, Beaton—Canada	32
1974	Coulehan et al.—Arizona	30
1974	Sabiston, Radomski—Canada	68
1974	Anderson et al.—Canada	25
	Average reduction in illness by vitamin C	44%

In 1976, Dr. Coulehan and his colleagues published a new study which produced headlines such as "Researchers Now Say Vitamin C Isn't Useful in Combating Colds." They concluded, "We do not believe that vitamin C has widespread usefulness as a cold remedy."

Their report published in the *New England Journal of Medicine* did note that the children on vitamin C had half the number of strep throats and slightly less illness time. The researchers doubted that this improvement justified a gram of vitamin C a day for life.

It should be noted that the incidence of colds for

both groups was much lower than expected, and it is possible that the boarding school for Navajo school-children in Arizona was not a real test of spreading cold viruses.

B-12 Scare

A report by Dr. Victor Herbert of Columbia University warned that large doses of vitamin C would destroy the body's supply of vitamin B-12 and cause serious nerve damage.[3] The warning stemmed from a crude test-tube experiment unrelated to body conditions, and later Dr. Jerome J. DeCrosse of the Medical College of Wisconsin proved this warning to have been a false scare.[4] Dr. DeCrosse found none of his patients who had received large amounts of vitamin C to be deficient in vitamin B-12, even though they were not taking vitamin B-12 supplements.

Additionally, Dr. Mehr Afronz and his colleagues at the St. Louis University Group Hospitals reported in the *Journal of the American Medical Association* in 1975 that they have been giving more than 4,000 milligrams of vitamin C daily to all spinal-cord-injury patients under their care, with no adverse effect on vitamin B-12 levels. They measured vitamin B-12 levels of their long-term patients, all of whom had been taking 4,000 milligrams of vitamin C for 11 months or more, and found not one patient deficient in vitamin B-12.[5]

Dr. James Greenwood, Chief of Neurosurgery at the Methodist Hospital in Houston, Texas, has also used large amounts of vitamin C for injuries and the preservation and protection of the spine and other joints. He too found no vitamin B-12 problem.

In addition, the analytical method for vitamin B-12 used by Dr. Herbert was inefficient for extracting the vitamin.[6]

Dr. Herbert later conceded that his results didn't reflect body conditions where the vitamins coexist.[7]

Kidney Stone Scare

Occasionally the claim is made that increased vitamin C intake increases the risk of kidney stones, but Drs. Charles E. Butterworth and Carlos Krundieck of the School of Medicine of the University of Alabama in Birmingham have reported that even taking 3,000 milligrams of vitamin C a day produces no increase in oxalates, the main material of kidney stones, in urine.[8]

Dr. Abram Hoffer of Victoria, British Columbia, writes me that in twenty years of experience of prescribing huge doses of vitamin C he has not seen any oxalate urinary stones in his patients.

Dr. Linus Pauling explained the harmlessness of vitamin C before the Senate Subcommittee on Health, chaired by Senator Edward Kennedy (D. Mass.) in 1975, as follows:

> Vitamin C has been described as one of the least toxic substances known. People have ingested 125 grams (over a quarter of a pound) at one time without harm, and an equal amount has been injected intravenously into a human being without harm. It is unlikely that ingestion in the amounts of two grams to twenty grams per day, the amounts [daily] synthesized by animals, over long periods of time would lead to harm. It has been suggested that a high intake of vitamin C continued for a long time might lead to the formation of kidney stones, but in fact not a single case has been reported in the medical literature . . . A careful study showed that the amount of oxalate was increased very little by an intake of four grams of vitamin C per day, and is only doubled for an intake of ten grams per day, for normal subjects.

Dr. W. J. McCormick published his finding that patients with urinary stones had, on average, a low level of vitamin C in their blood.[9]

Dr. Sherry Lewin makes similar statements about uric acid stones, "It is difficult to understand therefore, how such data can reasonably be used to indicate increased probability of formation of uric acid calculi [stones]."[10]

Kathryn E. Nickey, R.N. of the University of Tennessee College of Nursing, adds that vitamin C is effective in acidifying the urine of convalescing patients which provides protection against urinary infection and the formation of urinary stones. Bedridden patients are at higher risks of stones because of demineralization of the bones.

My own experience has indicated that the best protection against kidney stones is drinking large amounts of fluids so that the urine is clear (not necessarily colorless, but clear as opposed to cloudy) and staying free of extreme stress.

Cancer Scare

Dr. Richard San of the University of British Columbia was concerned because vitamin C damaged DNA in a test tube experiment. He was afraid that vitamin C in the body could lead to cancer.

If this were so, then vitamin C would not be allowed to be added to foods for enrichment because of the Delaney clause. As chapter Nine shows, vitamin C is cancer curative, not causative. Tests on living cells and animals have confirmed that vitamin C does not damage DNA in any way. This is another example as to why isolated test tube experiments are not valid tests for living systems.

There is a legitimate concern, however, that vitamin C can invalidate results of a once widely used test to detect bowel cancer. In fact, the possibility is open that megadoses of vitamin C could mess up any test, so always tell your physician how many vitamins you do take.

Tablet Deterioration

Vitamin C can be stored in closed bottles for five years or longer at room temperature without a significant loss in potency. Daily opening and closing causes less than a 2 percent loss over a period of twenty weeks. The breakdown products formed are the same formed in foods sitting in the grocery store, and are safe.

Sources

The main sources of vitamin C are fruits and vegetables. The citrus fruits (oranges, grapefruit, limes, and lemons), berries, melons, pineapple, guava, acerola cherries, rosehips, camu-camu, potatoes, leafy green vegetables, broccoli, green peppers, cabbage and tomatoes are important sources.

The acerola cherry is the richest source, followed by rosehips and camu-camu.

Table 16.2 lists some food values.

Table 16.2

VITAMIN C VALUES OF SOME FOODS

Food	mg/100 gm	Portion	mg/serving
Acerola, pulpy juice	1300	–	–
Green pepper, raw	128	1 med.	79
Broccoli, cooked	90	⅔ c	89
Brussel sprouts, cooked	87	⅔ c	75
Turnip greens, cooked	69	⅔ c	66
Kale, cooked	62	⅔ c	45
Strawberries, raw	59	⅔ c	58
Orange	50	1 med.	70
Mustard greens, cooked	48	⅔ c	45

Orange juice, frozen	45	1 c	112
Lemon juice	46	1 c	113
Grapefruit	38	½ med.	52
Grapefruit juice	38	1 c	84
Cabbage, cooked	33	⅔ c	37
Cantaloupe	33	¼ melon	32
Lime juice	32	1 c	80
Coleslaw	29	⅔ c	23
Spinach, cooked	28	⅔ c	33
Liver, beef, cooked	27	2 oz.	15
Tomato, raw	23	1 med.	34
Sweet potato, baked	22	1 med.	24
Peas, green, cooked	20	⅔ c	22
Potato, baked	20	1 med.	20
Tomato juice	16	1 c	39
Pineapple, canned	7	2 sm. sl.	8
Milk, whole	1	1 c	2
Beef, ground, cooked	0	3 oz.	0
Bread, white, enriched	0	1 sl.	trace
Butter	0	1 tbsp.	0
Egg	0	1 med.	0
Sugar, white	0	1 tsp.	0

U.S.D.A Handbook No. 8.

References

1. Cheraskin, E. et al. *J. Med. Assoc. of the State of Alabama*, 46:12, 39-40, 1977.

2. Pauling, Linus. *Vitamin C and the Common Cold*, San Francisco: W. H. Freeman, 1970.

3. Herbert, Victor and Jacob, Elizabeth. *J. Am. Mech. Assoc.*, 230:2, 241-242, 14 October 1974.

4. DeCrosse, Jerome J. *Surgery*, 79 608-612, 1975.

5. Afronz, Mehr. *J. Am. Med. Assoc.*, 232:2, 246, 21 April 1975.

6. Newmark, H. L. et al. *Amer. J. Clin. Nutr.*, 29:6, 645-649, June 1976.

7. Herbert, Victor. *Amer. J. Clin. Nutr.*, February 1978.

8. Butterworth, Charles and Krundieck, Carlos. *Amer. J. Clin. Nutr.*, April 1974.

9. McCormick, W. J. *The Medical Record*, 1946.

10. Lewin, Sherry. *Vitamin C: Its Molecular Biology and Medical Potential*. New York: Academic Press, 1976.

CHAPTER 17

Vitamin E

VITAMIN E (tocopherol) is a fat-soluble vitamin with no known toxicity. However, relatively large dosages of vitamin E should not be taken indiscriminately. Precaution is warranted for those with high blood pressure, diabetes and rheumatic heart disease, because approximately 30 percent of the people with these conditions have temporary rise in blood pressure. If the vitamin E dosage is increased slowly and moderately, this temporary increase is not usually observed. Also, people on any form of medication should inform their physician of any changes in their vitamin E intake. There is evidence that vitamin E lessens the need for insulin in diabetics and anticoagulants in heart patients; therefore, life-critical adjustments must be made in the dosages of these medicines.

The use of 400 to 1200 I.U. of vitamin E daily is considerably above the RDA, but such dosage has not produced observable harmful effects. Yet one has to keep in mind that vitamin E is fat-soluble and stored in the body, so some potential problem, either direct or indirect, is always a possibility.

There are differing forms of vitamin E. All of the

forms taken as a group are referred to as the "vitamin E complex" by some. It is probably more correct to say that several similar chemicals have vitamin E activity, rather than imply that one needs each of the forms to have complete vitamin E activity. However, we should realize that we still have a lot to discover about the action(s) of vitamin E in the body.

Tocopherol (the chemical name of vitamin E) exists in several structural forms called isomers: alpha, beta, gamma, and delta. Each has a different activity. This is why vitamin E capsules are labeled according to total activity (in International Units) rather than simply according to their weight (in milligrams).

Alpha-tocopherol biologically appears to be the most active isomer. Yet, in the test tube, delta-tocopherol has been found to be the superior antioxidant; thus one would expect delta-tocopherol to be the most active biologically. But delta-tocopherol is the least active biologically. Delta-tocopherol shows only 1 percent of the activity of alpha-tocopherol in the body.

The biological function of tocopherol in the body may be different from that in the test tube; it may have more functions than merely being an antioxidant. Remember: evidence has been found that it does indeed enter into enzymatic reactions and in electron transport.

Still another explanation for the varying levels of vitamin E activity among the different isomers is that some are broken down in the body faster and excreted more rapidly than others. Support for the argument that less efficient absorption from the intestine and a shorter biological half-life (period of action) are major factors in the lower potency of tocopherols other than alpha, is the fact that adding the other isomers directly to the blood yields higher than expected activity.

The prevailing thought at this time is that isomers other than alpha tocopherol contribute little to vitamin

E activity and thus are unimportant. What are Nature's purposes for the other isomers? Do we know all that there is to know? Do some isomers serve merely to protect other isomers?

There is more to consider than just which isomer or isomers of tocopherol to take.

When tocopherol is ingested, some of the activity (potency) may be lost before absorption, since this form (called the "free" or "available" form) is oxidized by air or in the gastrointestinal tract. Converting the "free" tocopherol to an organic salt of tocopherol, called an ester (acetate, succinate, etc.) protects its activity until it is in the body tissues and blood where you need it. It is in the stomach that the digestive process converts the esterified form, called tocopheryl, back into the biologically active tocopherol.

On a label, the name tocopheryl is followed by the name of the ester, as in tocopheryl acetate or tocopheryl succinate. It should be interpreted by the user as "stable tocopherol." The stomach will release the ester, thus tocopheryl becomes tocopherol again.

Knowing the isomer, ester and activity still doesn't tell most people all that they want to know. They want to know if it is natural or synthetic.

Each isomer can appear in two variations called enantiomorphs; one is designated "d," the other "l." Nature makes only the d-enantiomorph. Thus the body has evolved to use the d-variation. When tocopherols are made synthetically, a mixture of the d- and l- variation of each isomer is produced.

Each isomer thus can really have two asymmetric forms which are alike in every way except that their spatial molecular arrangements are such that they cannot be superimposed. The type of asymmetry involved is the same as exists between an object and its mirror image, or between one's two hands, which cannot be superimposed.

Isomers of this kind rotate the plane of polarized light in opposite directions. The two isomers are designated as d- and 1-, from the Latin prefixes "dextro-" and "levo-" designating right and left. The degree of rotation is called the "specific rotation" and is a characteristic property of a substance. Essentially all the amino acids found in nature are of the 1- form. This is an amazing fact, as we would offhand expect the two forms to be equally abundant. This illustrates the great importance of details of structure in living organisms.

Although enantiomorphs of a given compound have many of the same chemical properties, certain of their physical and essentially all of their biological properties are different, as discovered by Louis Pasteur in 1848. Body enzymes act on only one of a pair of enantiomorphs.

The presence of synthetic vitamin E is sometimes indicated without noting that it is the d1-form. Thus when we see the most active isomer, alpha tocopherol, written without the letter- prefix, we do not know if it is d-alpha tocopherol (the natural variation) or d1-alpha tocopherol (the synthetic variation). Since there is an advantage (natural vitamin E costs more) to listing d-alpha tocopherol, we can usually assume that when we do not see d- specified, it is the synthetic d1-alpha tocopherol.

We have now considered the main biological differences in the various forms of tocopherol, but we should also examine the differences in individual tolerances due to physical form.

Tocopherols are clear, viscous oils ranging in color from light yellow to red. When manufacturers prepare vitamin supplements, they not only have to choose which isomer, ester, enantiomorph and strength to use, but they must also keep in mind the composition of the rest of the formula.

As an example, adding tocopherol as an oil to a

powdery multivitamin and mineral mixture is undesirable. The tocopherol is readily attacked by inorganic iron and other antagonists, and the formulation becomes too tacky to coat as a pill. Thus a dry, protected form, such as micro-encapsulation with gelatin, is preferred.

Some people do not tolerate oils well and so prefer a dry form embedded either in acacia or gelatin.

Manufacturers sometimes prefer to dilute the tocopherol with wheat germ oil or another vegetable oil to more easily fill gelatin capsules. Larger capsules are produced than the mini-perles of the pure tocopherol products.

Thus a choice is possible in capsule size and shape, as well as presence of other oils.

Functions of Vitamin E

It is established that vitamin E is essential to human life, but debate exists as to what the functions of vitamin E are. Many contend that vitamin E is a general antioxidant to protect cell membranes and other body components against undesirable oxygen reactions (lipid peroxidation). Others contend that vitamin E is involved as an activator of enzymatic reactions, the synthesis of various prostaglandins (hormone-like compounds), and in ubiquinone (a biochemically important compound) reactions. Still others contend that both groups are right.

Vitamin E protects vitamins A and C against oxidation in the body. Vitamin E is required to protect the red blood cells from premature breakdown and, pharmacologically, it relieves the symptoms of intermittent claudication (painful or restless legs).[1]

Vitamin E was discovered by Drs. Herbert M. Evans and Katherine S. Bishop, who were pursuing the leads of Matthill and Conklin (1922). Evans and Bishop found a factor in lettuce leaves that prevented sterility in rats fed diets deficient in this factor. In 1936, Dr. Evans identified this factor as tocopherol. The sterility created by vitamin E deficiency becomes irreversible after certain physiological changes, but is reversible if caught early enough.

Some people have confused sterility with virility, and hence the widespread belief that vitamin E enhances sexual powers. Of course, if one *believes* vitamin E gives an assist, it will. In sexual matters particularly, the power of suggestion is most important.

Human studies with vitamin E deficiency have been limited because of ethical considerations and human tests with vitamin E against heart disease have often been discontinued before vitamin E would have time to correct the disease process. My studies have shown that vitamin E controls the synthesis of prostaglandins that repair blood platelets, and that this process just begins to show results after six months.

Vitamin E deficiencies in animals have led to many diseases, most of which seem to have human counterparts. The great number of diseases related to vitamin E is explained by the general involvement of vitamin E as an antioxidant or factor in prostaglandin production. Table 17.1 lists a number of the diseases in animals and humans related to vitamin E deficiency.

Because of negligible placental transfer, newborn animals, including human infants, have low tissue concentrations of vitamin E. Human milk is relatively rich in tocopherol content and meets the infants' requirement, whereas cows' milk is relatively low in vitamin E.

As the intake of polyunsaturates increases, the requirement for vitamin E also increases. Conditions interfering with fat absorption, such as pancreatic insufficiency, biliary tract diseases and mineral-oil ingestion, reduce the amount of vitamin E absorbed.

Deficiency Signs

These are not well established in humans. Pigmentation and anemia are perhaps early warnings. Other signs have been seen in animals, such as nutritional muscular dystrophy, testicle shrinkage and blood-vessel disorders.

Nutritional Status

Vitamin E had not been included in earlier nutritional surveys because RDAs were not established at that time. Since vitamin E is stripped out of grains during processing and not replaced in "enrichment," and Americans are consuming more and more processed foods, subclinical vitamin E deficiencies could be developing on a wide scale. Estimates of vitamin E intake show an average intake of 17 I.U., which means there are many people getting less than 17 I.U. or the RDA of 15 I.U., as well as those getting more.

Requirements

Without knowing all of the uses of vitamin E in the body, it is difficult to establish a Recommended Dietary Allowance.

The RDAs for 1968 and 1974 are as follows:

	1974	1968
Males, 11-14 years	12 I.U.	20 I.U.
15 plus	15	30
Females, 11 plus	12	25
Pregnant females	15	30
Lactating females	15	30
Children 1-3	7	10
4-6	9	10
7-10	10	15
Infants 0-0.5	4	5
0.5-1.0	5	5

I have found the Supernutrition points for women to be 400 I.U. and men 800 I.U.

The RDAs were reduced for no reason other than to match the amount in the average diet. The RDA committee reasoned that since the amount available did not produce recognizable deficiency symptoms, that amount must be sufficient. Of course the RDA committee doesn't consider cancer and heart disease as deficiency diseases.

Toxicity

No toxicity symptoms are known. Studies with growing turkeys have shown growth abnormalities at very high dosages. One physician has reported increased fatigue associated with vitamin E therapy. However, it seems to be an isolated report, as physicians commenting on this, have said that they find the opposite effect, that is, vitamin E therapy produces greater energy in their patients. If fatigue develops, have a doctor check the creatine level of blood and urine.

A 1977 report by Doctors Yank and Desai, published in the *Journal of Nutrition*, showed very massive amounts of vitamin E in rats produced depression in body weight, increase in relative heart and spleen weight, decrease in ash content of bones with concurrent increase in plasma alkaline phosphatase activity, reduced prothrombin time, and increased hematocrit values. At this time, it is not certain that the massive amount of vitamin E caused problems because of taste, and the diet was partially rejected by the rats or what.

Remember vitamin E is stored in the body and few people have needs exceeding 1600 I.U.

Precautions

As already mentioned, those wishing to take more vitamin E should increase their dosage slowly and gradually. Healthy people can change their vitamin E intake at will, but some people may have unknown borderline problems. Thus, a wise practice would be to increase at a rate of no more than 400 I.U. per two-week period.

Those with diabetes, high blood pressure or rheumatic heart disease should proceed at no more than 30 I.U. per month until they reach 400 I.U. Then they can proceed at 400 I.U. per month. They should monitor their blood pressure to make sure it doesn't increase.

All patients taking medication should check with their doctor.

Preferred Forms

Natural forms are preferred solely because there is a difference in the chemical molecules between synthetic and natural vitamin E. Although they show no difference—on an international unit basis—in antioxidant activity, we don't know about all functions of vitamin E. Since nature gives us only the natural d-isomer, rather than the man-made dl isomers, be safe and stick with the natural whenever possible.

My order of preference is as follows:
1) Mixed natural isomers
2) D-alpha tocopheryl succinate or D-alpha tocopheryl acetate
3) Dl-alpha tocopheryl succinate or Dl-alpha tocopheryl acetate

Dosage Advice

The vitamin is best absorbed if taken with meals or wheat germ oil (1 teaspoon or 2 to 3 capsules). Chelated iron or strongly bound organic forms of iron will not destroy vitamin E. The iron in food is chelated. Even when free (nonchelated) iron attacks vitamin E, the degradation product is still useful in most vitamin E functions in the body.

To double the blood level of vitamin E, the dosage must be increased forty times. Compared with the 100 I.U. level, 500 I.U. of vitamin E increases the blood level of vitamin E by only 9 percent.

Sources

Vitamin E occurs mainly in vegetables. Vegetable oils, if fresh, contain vitamin E, but it is lost rapidly. Leafy green vegetables and whole grains are the best sources. Although animal products contain little vitamin E, liver, heart, kidney, milk, and eggs are the best animal sources.

Table 17.1

VITAMIN E

Mechanisms

1. Antioxidant
2. Antiradical
3. Enzymatic (not well established)

Functions

1. Extends cell lifespan	6. Involved in heme synthesis
2. Improves blood oxygenation	7. Platelet protecting
3. Stimulates immune response	8. Membrane stabilizer
4. Involved in energy transport	9. Anti-clotting
5. Detoxifies free radicals	10. Prevents excessive scarring

Deficiency diseases helped by vitamin E

1. Heart disease	14. Arthritis
2. Intermittent claudication	15. Asthma
3. Aging	16. Emphysema
4. Senility	17. Encephalomalacia

5. Diabetes
6. Gangrene
7. Hypertension
8. Hypercholesterolemia
9. Glaucoma
10. Cataracts
11. Cancer protection
12. Muscular dystrophy
13. Liver necrosis
18. Hemolytic anemia
19. Steatitis
20. Embryonic degeneration
21. Exudative diathesis
22. Pancreatic atrophy
23. Menopause
24. Prostatitis
25. Burns
26. Infertility

References

1. Shute, Evan V. *The Heart and Vitamin E*. New Canaan, Connecticut: Keats Publishing, 1977.

CHAPTER 18

Selenium

THE most exciting news in nutrition that I have had the opportunity to watch has been to see selenium move from a laboratory curiosity to a supplement available in health food stores.

Needs Established

The latest news is that scientists are getting to agree upon just how much selenium is needed in man. The Ninth Revised Edition of the Recommended Dietary Allowances (RDAs) includes for the first time provisional recommendations for selenium. The recommendations are 50 to 200 micrograms (0.05 to 0.2 milligrams).

Unfortunately, the "average" diet probably contains only 25 to 60 micrograms of selenium. Those eating mostly processed foods and TV dinners have lower levels. Whole grains and eggs can be good sources of selenium, but my analyses of typical TV dinners have not found any detectable quantity.

Dr. Klaus Schwarz established selenium as an essential nutrient in 1957, but its function wasn't discovered until 1972.[1] Dr. John Rotruck and his colleagues at

the University of Wisconsin discovered that seleniwas a component of an enzyme involved in oxyg
transport.[2] Selenium can be thought of as an essent
partner of vitamin E. Without adequate selenium, vi
min E can't perform many of its functions. More rec
research indicates that there are additional duties f
selenium, such as in the regulation of some of the h
mone-like prostaglandins.

The importance of selenium to animals has long be
known. Animal nutritionists have supplemented anin
feed with selenium for decades. Selenium-deficient a
mals have a variety of debilitating diseases, includi
heart disease and nutritional muscular dystrophy.

Australia and New Zealand added selenium to ferizers to insure that feed crops would have adequate
lenium to wipe out the "white muscle disease" th
results from selenium deficiency.

In 1973, Canada added selenium to feeds for poul
and swine, and in April 1973, the FDA proposed ac
ing selenium to American feeds for poultry and swi
The order became effective in February 1974. T
FDA's April 1973 press release emphasized, "S
lenium deficiency in animals can result in decreas
rates of growth, disease, and death. Levels natura
found in animal feed vary widely depending on the s
in which the feed crops were grown. A recent survey
feed corn revealed that selenium content ranged from
low of 0.1 parts per million (ppm) to 2.03 ppm. It
estimated that 70 percent of the domestic corn a
soybeans used for animal feed does not have adequ
selenium to meet the animal's nutritional needs."

You can see the need for selenium supplements.
70 percent of the feed crops are deficient, it is a go
guess that 70 percent of all crops, plus more than
percent of meats are selenium deficient.

Geographical Distribution

Selenium, like iodine or cobalt, is lacking from some soils; or if it is present, it is in a form that makes it unavailable chemically for absorption into plant roots.

We are no longer conscious of the "Goiter Belt," which is a huge area in the midwest and Great Lake states, where the soil is deficient in iodine. Until we supplemented diets with iodine in the form of iodized salt, millions of Americans suffered the debilitating and disfiguring effects of goiter.

Cobalt-deficient soils led to vitamin B-12 deficiencies in animals, and hence man. Cobalt is required for the formation of vitamin B-12.

Now we regularly read of the studies that link regional selenium deficiencies with cancer and heart disease. Dr. Ray Shamberger of the Cleveland Clinic has noted that the lowest cancer rate is in Rapid City, South Dakota, where the people also have the highest selenium blood levels. Lima, Ohio, which had the lowest blood levels of selenium, also had the highest cancer rate, twice that of Rapid City. Other cities studied showed a similar correlation.[3] Of course, this is not definite proof of cause and effect.

In *Supernutrition for Healthy Hearts* I called attention to Dr. Shamberger's studies indicating that Americans living in selenium-deficient areas are three times more likely to die from heart disease than those living in selenium-rich areas.

The selenium-rich states of Texas, Oklahoma, Arizona, Colorado, Louisiana, Utah, Alabama, Nebraska and Kansas have the lowest heart disease rates. For example, Colorado Springs was 67 percent below the national heart disease death rate, and Austin was 53 percent below.

The selenium-deficient states, which include Connecticut, Illinois, Ohio, Oregon, Massachusetts, Rhode Island, New York, Pennsylvania, Indiana, Delaware and the District of Columbia, produce a heart disease death rate substantially higher than the national average.

Other selenium-deficient areas include parts of Washington, Florida, Michigan, Vermont, New Hampshire, and Maine.

Toxicity

Selenium was named after the moon goddess, Selene, but unlike the moon, selenium clearly shows two sides—a good side and a bad side. Selenium is essential, but becomes toxic at ten times the recommended intake.

Selenium tablets usually contain 50 micrograms each. The provisional RDA can be met with 1 to 4 tablets per day. Don't forget to allow for the 25 to 60 micrograms in the "average" diet. However, at the 1000 microgram (1 milligram) per day level, we come to the end of the safe range. This is equivalent to 20 tablets per day. Most people would find 2000 micrograms (40 tablets) daily to be toxic in a relatively short time. Follow label instructions or your doctor's recommendations.

Selenium supplements are only a problem when abused. As the FDA pointed out in its 27 April 1973 press release, "Tests have shown that animals absorb dietary selenium according to bodily needs, and rapidly excrete any excess."

One or two popular nutritionists have wrongly said that selenium causes cancer. This is definitely not true, as reported by the FDA in the Federal Register (V39 #5, January 8 1974). The FDA said that several adequate and well-controlled investigations found no tumor activity for selenium. As mentioned earlier, there are considerable data to show that selenium may be protective against cancer. The misinformation arises from old studies in which "the selenium-treated rats lived longer than the control animals, and the [non-malignant] tumor incidence may therefore have been due to the increased lifespan."

Good natural sources of selenium include garlic, onion, asparagus, mushrooms, eggs, brewer's yeast, tuna, liver, shrimp, kidney, meat, wheat and corn. Of course, the foods vary in selenium content according to their source of nutrients: plants with the soil content, and meats with the feed content. Consequently, there is no point in reporting typical food values—there are none. The refining and cooking of food cause serious losses of selenium. Typically, each process destroys one-half of the original content. TV dinners, raw fruits and vegetables are usually very low in selenium.

Very few of us get adequate selenium now, and selenium is being depleted rapidly from soils. Since research strongly indicates that selenium deficiency increases the probability of cancer and heart disease, supplements must be considered. To prevent cancer, adequate amounts of the major antioxidant nutrients must be taken—vitamin A, vitamin C, vitamin E, and selenium.

References

1. Schwarz, Klaus. *J. Amer. Chem. Soc.*, 79:3292-3293, 1957.

2. Rotruck, John. *Science*, 179:588, 1973.

3. Shamberger, Raymond. Sixtieth Annual Meeting of the Federation of American Societies for Experimental Biology. Anaheim, California, April 1976.

Part Four
PERSONAL STRATEGY

CHAPTER 19

What You Can Do

LET's put all of the scientific findings about the causes of cancer and the protection of various nutrients into practical use. Just what can you do to prevent or help control cancer?

First of all, let's get rid of *unnecessary* fear, and have a healthy respect for what should be feared. There is no need to be a fanatic and try to avoid all cancer-causing substances. But on the other hand, how wise is it to start the day with a cigarette and saccharin-sweetened coffee, complete with an additive-laddered cream substitute with cereal that is rich in artificial coloring and all sorts of additives? Why not try food?

This is not to say that you can't have dyed and additive-rich plastic foods at a friend's house on a rare occasion. But there is no need to buy the worst examples at the store and bring it into your home for regular consumption.

Practice Good Health Habits

The watchwords of good health are moderation and common sense. Learn from the groups that emphasize well-balanced diets, exercise, rest and moderation in the use or avoidance of tobacco, alcohol, coffee, tea and addictive drugs. As St. Thomas Aquinas once said in 1261, *"In Medio Virtus Stat,"* which literally translated means, "Virtue stands in the middle way" or more freely "Moderation in all things."

Remember the lower cancer rates of the Mormons reported by Dr. James E. Enstrom of the School of Public Health of the University of California at Los Angeles. Mormons comprise some 73 percent of the 1.1 million people in Utah, whose rate of death from cancer is the lowest for any state in the nation and overall death rate is second only to Hawaii. The state's rate of death from all cancer is about 25 percent less than the national rate. In Utah County, which is 90 percent Mormon, the death rate from all cancers is 35 percent less than the national rate for males and 38 percent less for females. In 1970, the crude death rate (total deaths divided by total population) for Mormons in Utah was 33 percent less than that of non-Mormons; the same rate (for Mormons contrasted with non-Mormons) was 40 percent less in Idaho, 48 percent less in California, and 51 percent less in Nevada.

Still further data come from an all-California study based on Mormon church records for 1970. The study of 350,000 California Mormons showed the observed mortality for cancer was about half the expected mortality for all causes and for all cancer sites. For several cancer sites, the observed mortality was substantially less than half the expected mortality. Particularly interesting is the low observed mortality for cancer sites such as stomach, colon, rectum, breast, uterus, prostate, kidney and lymphomas. None of these cancers has been clearly related to risk factors like smoking and drinking.

As emphasized in chapter Five, these same Mormons eat more meat than the national average. So don't confuse Mormons with vegetarians. The biggest difference in lifestyle between Mormons and most non-Mormons is in their tendency toward moderation, good nutrition and the avoidance of alcohol and tobacco.

And guess what—they enjoy life! Moderation doesn't require giving up the things of real value. It only means that you shouldn't make a fool of yourself and a wreck of your body by overindulgence.

In 1974, Dr. Lester Breslow of the University of California reported on a five-and-one-half-year study of 7,000 Californians. Dr. Breslow and his colleagues studied seven health habits and found that people who get adequate sleep, eat breakfast, stay lean, avoid empty calorie snacks, don't smoke, exercise regularly, and abstain from or go easy with alcohol are rewarded with superior health.[1]

Dr. Breslow concluded, "The physical health of men in their mid-fifties who follow six or seven [of the above listed] good health habits is on the average about the same as men twenty years younger who follow three or fewer of the good health habits.

"Those who followed all of the good practices were in better health at every age than those who followed one or few. Poor health habits were more closely related to mortality than was income."

Each of the seven good habits individually are effective, but it is possible that they do have synergistic value because one bad habit doesn't strain a body system to weaken its defense against the next bad habit. In other words, the bad habits most likely are synergistic in destroying health, and the good habits merely prevent this negative synergism from occurring. Here are the comments about each health habit.

Smoking: The risk of cancer parallels the number of cigarettes smoked.

Weight: A few percent above ideal weight isn't critical, but being 20 percent over one's ideal weight increases the death rate.

Exercise: Those who exercise regularly have a mortality rate of only about half as high as those who never exercise.

Drinking: Heavy drinkers (especially five drinks or more a day) have higher death rates.

Snacking: those who snack on empty calories (junk food) or have erratic eating patterns have poorer health.

Breakfast: Those who eat breakfast regularly have better health.

Sleep: Men who sleep between seven and eight hours daily have a lower mortality than men receiving more or less sleep. For women, the ideal sleeping time is seven hours or a little less.

Dr. Breslow's study indicates that for men aged forty-five following six or seven of the good health habits, the additional life expectancy would average 33.1 years to age 78.1. For a 45-year-old man following none-to-three of the good health habits, the average additional life expectancy would be only 21.6 years to the age of 66.6. Not only would a forty-five-year-old man live twelve years longer by improving three or four health habits, but he would be in much better health till the end.

An interesting experiment was performed by Dr. Hans Kugler, author of *Slowing the Aging Process* (Pyramid, 1973) and *Dr. Kugler's Seven Keys to a Longer Life* (Stein and Day, 1977).

Dr. Kugler used three groups of mice to make a point about controlling health with good habits. Group one, the control group, received a balanced diet for mice, tap water, and a normal experimental environment. Group two received special treatment such as "mega" doses of vitamins and minerals, forced exercise, toys and private quarters, and other special treatment. Group three was what Dr. Kugler called his "average businessmen;" this group received 20 percent refined sugar in their diet, were regularly exposed to cigarette smoke, received the equivalent of three alcoholic drinks per day and did no exercise.

The "average businessmen" group of mice had a lifespan 30 percent shorter than the control group and 50 percent shorter than the privileged group. The differences in lifespans were mainly due to different cancer rates.

Dr. Kugler performed another experiment to answer "experts" who claim that "negligible" amounts of carcinogens do not present health hazards. He subjected one group of mice to a mixture of "safe" quantities of nitrates, nitrites, DES, saccharin and Chicago tap water, while giving the control group of mice bottled spring water in place of the above. The mice receiving the "safe" amounts of the chemicals had an average lifespan 20 percent shorter than the controls, mainly due to an increase in cancer.

Dr. Edith Weir of the USDA estimated in 1971 that better nutrition (and she was speaking of RDA levels, not megadoses) would save 150,000 lives from cancer each year. In 1975, I projected that supernutrition would reduce the cancer death rate by 30 to 40 percent. I now find that to be a conservative projection. Especially when the incidence of at least some cancers can be reduced by 80 to 90 percent with selenium.

Here are some specific examples of steps to take to lower the risk of cancer.

Cancer Prevention .

We must first of all practice supernutrition and then try

to reduce our exposure to cancer-causing agents. A happy, positive attitude will be important.

A supernutrition plan against cancer includes a diverse and well-balanced diet, with as many fresh, unprocessed foods as possible, as well as few junk foods as possible. The diet should therefore be a natural high fiber diet containing bran, pectin and cellulose.

The following supplements may prove to be helpful to you, but check with your physician and remember that each of us has different needs and different limits.

Retinol	Vitamin A	10,000 to	35,000 I.U.
Ascorbic Acid	Vitamin C	750 to	2,000 mg.
Tocopherol	Vitamin E	400 to	800 mg.
Selenium	–	150 to	200 mcg.
Thiamine	Vitamin B-1	50 to	100 mg.
Riboflavin	Vitamin B-2	50 to	100 mg.
Niacin	Vitamin B-3	40 to	100 mg.
Pantothenic Acid	Vitamin B-5	50 to	200 mg.
Pyridoxine	Vitamin B-6	20 to	100 mg.
Cyanocobalamin	Vitamin B-12	20 to	100 mcg.
Pangamic Acid	(Vitamin B-15)	25 to	50 mg.
Choline		40 to	100 mg.
Inositol		10 to	75 mg.
Folic Acid		0.1 to	0.8 mg.
Paba		10 to	50 mg.
Iodine		0.1 to	0.2 mg.
Zinc		5 to	15 mg.

Acidophilus (Lactobacillus Acidophilus) (one capsule daily)

Again I stress these are not specific recommendations for any individual, but are average levels by which to judge your personal supplement program. My own needs are even higher than I have outlined here for the mythical "average" person. Perhaps your needs are lower. Work with your physician to determine your specific needs. I have devoted portions of my earlier books, *Supernutrition: Megavitamin Therapy* and *Supernutrition for Healthy Hearts*, to the subject of how to determine your specific needs.

The next part of your prevention strategy is to reduce your exposure to cancer-causing agents. The rules are:

- Don't smoke
- Eat fresh, unprocessed foods as often as possible
- Drink filtered or good quality bottled water
- Avoid foods colored with artificial colors
- Eat very little nitrite-preserved processed meats
- If living in a polluted area, move to a less polluted area
- Avoid chemically fractionated foods (foods from which part of the whole has been removed: e.g. fiber from wheat)
- Avoid foods having long lists of added chemicals
- Avoid too many fats—especially unsaturated fats
- Avoid carcinogens in your work environment
- Exercise regularly—this improves your immune system and stimulates hormone metabolism
- Avoid X rays unless absolutely critical
- Don't overdo sun bathing, wear wide-brimmed hats in the sunlight, and use PABA as a sunscreen if you are light-complexioned
- Wash raw foods thoroughly
- Avoid aerosol sprays
- Avoid using pesticides unless as a last resort
- Avoid saccharin
- Don't take medicine needlessly
- Learn to enjoy life
- Air out dry-cleaned clothes before wearing
- Air out new plastics before using (vinyl chloride)
- Avoid products containing asbestos (including some talcum powders. Use corn starch powders instead)
- Take extra vitamin E on polluted days
- Eat lots of garlic—it contains the anticancer compounds alliin and allicin
- Take frequent, long, hot baths to improve the oxygen supply to all cells

Controlling Cancer

To win over cancer, make the commitment to fight it. *You* can beat cancer. More than anything else it takes your determination to win and faith. Start now by telling your cancer that you will beat it and that *it* is starting to lose. Every day reinforce your determination by concentrating your mental powers on the cancer to let it know it is losing more each day.

Conquering cancer requires a wholistic approach. Take any conventional therapy you wish and add all of the supplements listed under the preceding section on preventing cancer.

In addition, add the following or increase those previous supplements to the levels indicated below.

Ascorbic Acid	Vitamin C	additional 10,000 to 30,000 milligrams
Tocopherol	Vitamin E	additional 400 I.U.
Dessicated liver tablets		per label
Pangamic Acid	Vitamin B-15	additional 100 mg
Hydrochloric Acid tablets (aids digestion)		per label
Amino Acid tablets or powdered protein		25 to 75 grams
Bromelain (digestive enzyme)		per label
Laetrile		12 grams intravenously
Pancreatic Enzymes		2 to 4 tablets with each meal, plus at midday and before bed
Chelated minerals		per label
Potassium tablets		per label

Yogurt	almost daily
Seeds	daily
Asparagus	often

Don't neglect the long hot baths every day. With your physician's approval and further study on the subject, take occasional coffee or vitamin C colonics (enemas). Keep up to date on the progress of Laetrile research and other nutritional therapies since the printing of this book by joining one or more of the cancer societies for the general public, or write to them for the latest information. Also a list of doctors using Laetrile therapy and other nutritional therapies can be obtained by sending a self-addressed, stamped return envelope to any of the following organizations.

Committee for Freedom of Choice in Cancer Therapy, Inc.
146 Main St., Suite 408
Los Altos, CA 94022

Cancer Control Society
2043 N. Berendo
Los Angeles, CA 90027

National Health Federation
212 W. Foothill Blvd.
Monrovia, CA 91016

International Association of Cancer Victors and Friends
Box 707
Solona Beach, CA 92075

Arlin J. Brown Information Center
Box 251
Ft. Belvoir, VA 22060

International Academy of Preventive Medicine
10409 Town and Country Way, Suite 200
Houston, TX 77024

Also consider stimulating your immune system with BCG injections. (BCG is a drug used for tuberculosis.) A list of physicians experienced with BCG therapy for cancer can be obtained by sending a self-addressed, stamped return envelope to:

Research Foundation
70 W. Hubbard St.
Chicago, IL 60610

Also check with the previous organizations for the latest information on heat therapy. It is believed to be very effective in Europe and Mexico. Cancer cells have a poor blood supply and do not dissipate heat as well as normal cells, so they are more vulnerable to heat. Heat therapy, it is thought, directed to the region of the cancer kills cancer cells without injuring normal cells. A few research centers are starting to use it in the United States.

Start enjoying life again, even if you have severe pain. Remember—mind over matter. With willpower, the brain can manufacture its own pain-killing opiates. For severe pain at present, the Brompton's Cocktail can be used which consists of cocaine (legal for medical use), morphine and antiemetics (to prevent vomiting). This is recommended in *Science*, 25 November 1977.

Your own determination to do daily battle against your cancer is your best weapon. Reread chapter Nine on vitamin C. Read the other books on nutritional therapies against cancer. *You* can do it, just as so many thousands of others have. I know it works.

Again I stress that you must not attempt to treat yourself. Your physician will not be insulted—what if he is? It's your life—if you ask to be referred to an expert in your type of cancer.

Work with your family physician and the cancer specialist, and encourage them to consult a physician specializing in nutritional therapy. A list of such physicians can be obtained from the various organizations previously listed in this chapter.

You deserve the best guidance available, but the final decision rests with you. Under no circumstance should you treat yourself first, then seek professional help after it's too late. Nor should you accept medicine or treatment from anyone other than a licensed professional of the healing arts. Freedom is ours only as long as we use it wisely. As a team, your physicians and you can utilize the best of standard therapy and nutritional therapy to overcome cancer.

Equally important is your dedication and will to defeat the cancer. Faith, love and peace of mind will help you in your battle. Read the success testimonials of others in the various books on cancer. Another good book that I have not mentioned before is *Thank God I Have Cancer* by Rev. Clifford Oden.[2] Rev. Oden defeated cancer with nutritional therapy, and his battle led him to a deeper understanding of human health and happiness.

OK! Tell your cancer where it can go, and get to work. Keep the faith. I would appreciate a letter from you after you win your battle.

References

1. Breslow, Lester and Belloc, Nedra. *Prev. Med.,* 1:409-421, 1972.

2. Oden, Clifford. *Thank God I Have Cancer.* Los Altos, California: Choice Publications, 1977.

1983: LOOKING BACK—
AND AHEAD

It is a great pleasure to see the medical community begin to understand the preventive and therapeutic role of diet in cancer. In 1978, when this book was first published, only a small segment of the scientific community was aware that certain nutrients could inhibit the cancer process. Since that time, additional research has confirmed the results reported in this book. I have been able to add this information at the end of key chapters in this revision.

Today, the big news in cancer prevention and protection is that government health agencies and the medical community are finally beginning to recognize that nutrients are, if not the answer, at least an important part of the solution. The world at large is even beginning to be aware that it is possible for the body to develop an immunity to existing cancer. Major chemical studies on the role of nutrients as protection against human cancer are under way, and plans have been announced to test these same nutrients as added therapy to treat cancer. Reports have been written of successful small-scale (100 patients) studies showing that these nutrients have been successful.

The government is declaring its interest: The National Academy of Sciences advises everyone to include ample quantities of the protective nutrients to reduce the risk of cancer. The National Cancer Institute has given Linus Pauling, the two-time Nobel Prize winner, a fund for research on the function of vitamin C as a cancer antagonist.

All this is a long way from 1963, when my research on these nutrients was just beginning. I became interested in oxidation reactions, which are chemical reactions involving "corrosive" elements such as oxygen, chlorine or fluorine. Although I was working with industrial materials, I was also interested in oxidation problems in the body that led to poor performance, particularly in athletes.

This research led to the study of free radicals, the highly active molecular fragments that can cause great harm to living systems. Few people in those days had ever heard of free radicals. Today you see them mentioned in popular magazines such as *Reader's Digest*.[1] Free radicals can speed up aging and spark the cancer process initiated by chemicals or radiation and possibly other agents. Later research revealed that free radicals can also help start the formation of deposits in the arteries that cause heart disease.

Vitamin E and the other antioxidant nutrients under study turned out to protect the body against the harmful free radicals. My experiments showed the antiradicals, A, C, and E and the trace mineral selenium to be protectors against cancer, heart disease and aging.

Test-tube studies of antioxidants were concentrated on the effects of synergism, that is, finding whether certain combinations of nutrients would prove more effective than individual nutrients. Ultraviolet radiation was used to provoke free-radical reactions in polyunsaturated fats in a gelatin base. Then the protective action of the antiradicals would be measured by determining the amount of polymerization or cross-linking of the gelatin molecules by gas chromatography and melting-point studies.

In 1968 Dr. Denham Harman reported his brillant study that showed individual antioxidants extended the lifespans of laboratory animals.[2] However, the great quantities required of any of the antioxidants prevented practical use for humans. For example, the results achieved by Dr. Harman required that one-half of one percent of the diet be vitamin E. Aside from the cost and difficulty of downing that much E, there was a small chance of toxicity from such large doses.

As mentioned in chapter 10, I began studies to find out whether a combination of nutrients was less toxic than large doses of single ones. The final combination was chosen not only because it worked so well, but also because it provided protection against toxicity of some component nutrients.

Laboratory animal experiments proved that the synergistic combination worked. The total effect was better than any achieved by single ingredients or combination in less amounts than worked in the experiments. On October 23, 1970, I described my experiments before the International Gerontology Congress in Toronto, Canada.[3] *Chemical and Engineering News* and Reuters news agency published the results of my experiments in 1970.[4,5] In 1971, *Medical World News* and *Prevention* published perhaps the first mention of free radicals and selenium in non-chemical magazines.[6,7] I decided to patent this combination of antioxidants so that I could be assured of sponsorship of the expensive human clinical trials that would have to be conducted to bring my discovery to the public. The first patents in this series were filed in late 1969 and 1970.[8] On December 8, 1970, I applied for Investigational New Drug Status for my formulation with the Food and Drug Administration. It was denied pending further research.

Further discoveries followed. The combination of nutrients seemed to prevent cancer and was effective against cancer already present because it stimulated the immune system. It was also found that some single antioxidants did not always prevent cancer, but sometimes simply shifted the site of the cancer. When mice were given a chemical that usually causes stomach cancer, some single antioxidants shifted the cancer site to the pancreas. Additional patents were filed in 1972.[9]

My synergistic combination, however, would provide protective action at all sites. Further research details were published in an article entitled "Cancer: New Directions" in *American Laboratory*[10], and also in Dr. Hans Kugler's book, *Slowing The Aging Process*.[11]

In 1975 I reported my research in *Supernutrition*, my first book for the general audience.[12]

On February 2 and 3, 1978, the National Cancer Institute held a workshop on chemoprevention of cancer, discussing the antioxidants of my patents.[13]

By 1980, the nutritional scientists had gained some respect from the conservatives. A successful 100-patient clinical trial at a Missouri veterans' hospital showed that antioxidants could inhibit cancer.[14] The National Cancer Institute on September 15 sponsored a symposium entitled "Lipid Oxidation, Vitamin E, Selenium and Carcinogenesis"[15]. This symposium centered on how vitamin E and selenium prevented a certain type of oxidation that can cause cancer.

More scientists were attracted to this area of research. In 1981, the pace quickened.

In January 1981 the American Cancer Society's *Courier,* the newsletter of the units, branches and committees of the New York City ACS, carried an article entitled "Nutrition and Cancer: A Matter of Prudence."[16] The newsletter commented, "Vitamins are important, especially in view of the fact that chronic deficiencies of vitamins A, C, and E, as well as most of the B-complex vitamins, have been shown to increase the susceptibility of animals to chemically induced tumors. Vitamins have been found to give smokers some protection against lung cancer; vitamin C enhances the body immune response to several diseases, including cancer. In a recent experiment in Kansas, vitamin C therapy reduced the number of leukemia cells among a group of leukemia patients by an average of 79 percent.

Vitamin E is known to negatively affect chemically induced tumor incidence. Selenium, an antioxidant, does its anticancer work by preventing 'free radicals' (a very reactive fragment of a molecule) from damaging healthy cells.''

The article also commented, ''Ten years ago . . . if a university scientist told a public forum how to help prevent cancer by eating more wisely, he might in short order find himself shot with ridicule. That was ten years ago. Just a few months ago, not one, but a whole battery of scientists and physicians stood before a meeting about cancer and nutrition sponsored by the University of California at San Francisco whence it became evident that the new age of cancer prevention through better diet is here.''

The American Cancer Society article also quoted Dr. Jan van Eys: ''Nutrition is an uneasy science for the medical profession. It is essential that the reawakening of interest in nutrition is not again translated into just dietetics . . . There is no doubt that nutrition is the next major adjuvant modality in cancer therapy . . . The scope, utility, safety and pathophysiologic basis of this treatment deserves the same scientific approach as that being given to [other advances]. We should fervently hope that we will have the wisdom to approach the problem scientifically.''

Science, the official magazine of the American Association for the Advancement of Science, published a report on May 1, 1981, about glutathione, a natural sulfur-containing food component which cured liver cancer in mice; it is one of the group of our antioxidants.[17]

In the same month, the National Cancer Institute held a chemoprevention workshop at which the leading candidates for cancer prevention were presented as vitamins A, C and E and the trace mineral selenium.[18]

However, a July 29, 1981, meeting between the National Cancer Institute and Life Science Laboratories Inc., on the subject of successful experiments using synergistic antioxidants to prevent and cure cancer, resulted in little additional progress. The NCI wanted more animal tests, more autopsies, and more development and application of the theory before supporting it to any significant degree.

On March 31, 1982, the *Medical Tribune* noted that the worldwide growth of scientific information on the role of vitamins as cancer inhibitors had reached "critical mass."[19]

On June 16, 1982, the National Academy of Sciences advised that people include more vitamins A, C and E and selenium in their diet.[20] One week later, the National Cancer Institute and four other government agencies held the first Conference on Radioprotectors and Anticarcinogens[21]. Scientists from around the world discussed the role of free radicals in cancer and the protective effects of antioxidants.

On June 30, 1982, the *Medical Tribune* reported that "combination vitamin therapy, or vitamin-antioxidant therapy, may turn out to be the way to go in cancer chemoprevention in high-risk populations and in the treatment of pre-cancerous lesions."[22] This conclusion was reached after weighing the new evidence presented at the First International Conference on the Modulation and Medication of Cancer by Vitamins.

In the same issue of the *Medical Tribune*, the then Secretary of Health and Human Services, Richard S. Schweiker, stated: "In the laboratory, many of the micronutrients found in our diet—vitamin A precursors, vitamins C and E, selenium and certain chemicals appear to act as cancer-preventive agents."

On November 15, 1982, the *Wall Street Journal* reported "Such nutrients as selenium, vitamins A, C and E, to name a few, may block the mysterious process by which a normal cell turns malignant. . . . the National Cancer Institute's scientific advisors now are mulling over 49 proposals for new studies of possible inhibitors . . . the proposals . . . cover the use of a dozen or more food constituents in inhibiting cancer."[23]

In December 1982, the International Study Center for Environmental Health Sciences held a symposium on cancer causation and prevention.[24] Nutrient protection against free radicals was the major topic. At that time, Life Science Laboratories, Inc. decided to expand on my nutritional research and announced that they would sponsor clinical trials to demonstrate the effectiveness of the antioxidant combination.

Walter Ross, editor of *Cancer News,* an American Cancer Society publication, gave an excellent summary of the role of diet in cancer in the February 1983 *Reader's Digest.*[1] He pointed out that as natives of a country migrate to new lands and assume new diets and lifestyles, the major types of cancer that they suffer change, as well as their overall cancer rate. Several studies have monitored the changes in bowel and stomach cancer after the Japanese arrived in Hawaii and then California.

Mr. Ross also quoted noted cancer researcher Dr. Richard Doll as indicating that U.S. cancer deaths could be reduced by a third through dietary changes. Evidence is given in this book to indicate that certain types of cancer—such as breast, stomach, bowel and pancreas—can be reduced to one-tenth of their current level by dietary changes.

Mr. Ross also reported that the National Cancer Institute and the American Cancer Society were funding medical research into the chemoprevention of cancer, emphasizing "natural inhibitors vitamins A, C and E, beta-carotene and the trace mineral selenium, and . . . on certain chemical cousins of vitamin A."

As this edition is going to press, the American Oil Chemists Society is conducting a course for scientists entitled, "Cancer: A Molecular Event. Lipid Oxidation, Antioxidants, Selenium and the Etiology of Cancer."[25] Lecturers for this course are from the National Institutes of Health, U.S. Department of Agriculture Nutrition Institute, Duke University, University of California, University of Illinois, University of Minnesota, the Cleveland Clinic, Roswell Park Memorial Institute and others.

The information in this book will bring you up to date

on the research linking diet and cancer. Some of us do not have the luxury of waiting for all the results to come in from the clinical trials now under way.

As the National Academy of Sciences panel chairman, Dr. Clifford Grobstein of the University of California, emphasized when the panel's report was issued in June 1982: "The evidence is increasingly impressive that what we eat does affect our chances of getting cancer, especially particular kinds of cancer. We should try to put what is learned to use as soon as possible to avoid any unnecessary delay in taking preventive action."[20]

In any event, I am proud that I have had the opportunity to initiate some of the research that has brought us this far and have brought this information to the public in spite of the vicious harassment from a few who resist the truth.

So now in the 80s, the concept that one of the greatest threats to life in the twentieth century can be defeated by non-dangerous means is well on its way to firm ground. It can only go forward!

References

1. Ross, W. *Reader's Digest* 78–82, Feb. 1983.

2. Harman, D. *J. Gerontol.* 23(4) 476–482 (1968).

3. Passwater, R. 23rd Annual Meeting of the Gerontological Society (Oct. 21–24, 1970), Toronto.

   Also see the *Gerontologist* 10(3) 11, 28 (1970).

4. Anon. *Chem. Eng. News* 48:17 (Oct. 26, 1970).

5. Anon. Reuters News Agency (Oct. 23, 1970).

6. Fishbein, M. *Med. World News* 52 (June 4, 1971).

7. Anon. *Prevention* 23 (12) 104–110 (Dec. 1971).

8. Passwater, R. US 39140 and others.

9. Passwater, R. US 97011 and others.

10. Passwater, R. *Amer. Lab* 5(6) 10–22 (1973).

11. Kugler, H. *Slowing Down the Aging Process*, Pyramid, NY (1973).

12. Passwater, R. *Supernutrition: Megavitamin Revolution*, Dial Press, NY (1975).

13. Workshop on Chemoprevention of cancer. (Carcinogenesis Research Program, Div. Cancer Cause and Prevention, NCI (Feb. 2 & 3, 1978).

14. Donaldson, R. National Cancer Institute, May 9, 1983. Also: Annual Meeting of V. A. Surgeons 1980

15. Lipid Oxidation, Vit. E, Selenium and Carcinogenesis Workshop-National Cancer Institute, Bethesda, MD (Sept. 15–16, 1980).

16. Anon. Nutr. and Cancer, *ACS Courier*, NY (Jan. 1981).

17. Novi, A. *Science* 212 (4494) 541–543 (May 1, 1981).

18. Chemoprevention Workshop, National Cancer Institute, Bethesda, MD (May 21–22, 1981).

19. Anon. *Med. Tribune* (March 31, 1982).

20. *Diet, Nutrition and Cancer*. National Academy of Sciences, Washington, D.C. (June 1982).

21. First Conference on Radioprotectors & Anticarcinogens, National Bureau of Standards, Gaithersburg, MD (June 21–24, 1982).

22. Anon. *Med. Tribune* (June 30, 1982).

23. Bishop, J. *Wall St. Journal* 1 (Nov. 15, 1982).

24. Cancer and the Environment Symposium. Cancer Causation and Prevention: Biochemical Mechanisms. Internat. Study Center for Environ. Health Sciences, Wash., D.C. (Dec. 13–15, 1982).

25. Cancer: A Molecular Event. Lipid Oxidation, Antioxidants, Selenium and the Etiology of Cancer. American Oil Chemists' Society—Lake Geneva, WI (May 5–7, 1983).

Bibliography and Additional Reading

Cameron, Ewan. *Hyaluronidase and Cancer*. Elmsford, New York: Pergamon Press, 1966.

Clark, Linda. *Know Your Nutrition*. New Canaan, Connecticut: Keats Publishing, 1973.

Culbert, Michael L. *Freedom From Cancer*. New York: Pocket Books, 1977.

Fredericks, Carlton. *Breast Cancer: A Nutritional Approach*. New York: Grosset & Dunlap, 1977.

Gerson, Max. *A Cancer Therapy*. Delmar, California: Totality Press, 1958.

Hoffer, A. and Walker, Morton. *Orthomolecular Nutrition*. New Canaan, Connecticut: Keats Publishing, 1978.

Kittler, Glenn D. *Laetrile—Control for Cancer*. New York: Warner Paperback Library, 1963.

Kugler, Hans. *Seven Keys to a Longer Life*. New York: Stein and Day, 1978.

——————— *Slowing Down the Aging Process*. New York: Jove, 1975.

Oden, Clifford. *Thank God I Have Cancer!* Los Altos, California: Choice Publications, 1977.

Passwater, Richard A. *Supernutrition: Megavitamin Revolution*. New York: Pocket Books, 1976.

——————— *Supernutrition for Healthy Hearts*. New York: Jove, 1978.

Pauling, Linus. *Vitamin C and the Common Cold*. San Francisco: W. H. Freeman, 1970.

Pfeiffer, Carl C. *Mental and Elemental Nutrients*. New Canaan, Connecticut: Keats Publishing, 1975.

——————*Zinc and Other Micro-Nutrients*. New Canaan, Connecticut: Keats Publishing, 1978.

Shute, Evan V. *The Heart and Vitamin E*. New Canaan, Connecticut: Keats Publishing, 1977.

Shute, Wilfrid E. *The Complete, Updated Vitamin E Book*. New Canaan, Connecticut: Keats Publishing, 1975.

Stone, Irwin. *The Healing Factor: Vitamin C Against Disease*. New York: Grosset & Dunlap, 1972.

Index

Index

257